Rivers: A Very Short Introduction

VERY SHORT INTRODUCTIONS are for anyone wanting a stimulating and accessible way in to a new subject. They are written by experts and have been translated into more than 40 different languages. The series began in 1995 and now covers a wide variety of topics in every discipline. The VSI library contains nearly 400 volumes—a Very Short Introduction to everything from Indian philosophy to psychology and American history—and continues to grow in every subject area.

Very Short Introductions available now:

Nick Middleton

RIVERS

A Very Short Introduction

OXFORD
UNIVERSITY PRESS

OXFORD
UNIVERSITY PRESS

Great Clarendon Street, Oxford ox2 6DP

Oxford University Press is a department of the University of Oxford.
It furthers the University's objective of excellence in research, scholarship,
and education by publishing worldwide in

Oxford New York

Auckland Cape Town Dar es Salaam Hong Kong Karachi
Kuala Lumpur Madrid Melbourne Mexico City Nairobi
New Delhi Shanghai Taipei Toronto

With offices in

Argentina Austria Brazil Chile Czech Republic France Greece
Guatemala Hungary Italy Japan Poland Portugal Singapore
South Korea Switzerland Thailand Turkey Ukraine Vietnam

Oxford is a registered trade mark of Oxford University Press
in the UK and in certain other countries

Published in the United States
by Oxford University Press Inc., New York

British Library Cataloguing in Publication Data

Data available

Library of Congress Cataloging in Publication Data

Data available

Typeset by SPI Publisher Services, Pondicherry, India
Printed in Great Britain by
Ashford Colour Press Ltd, Gosport, Hampshire

ISBN 978-0-19-958867-1

3 5 7 9 10 8 6 4

This book is for Cherry

Contents

List of illustrations

Introduction

Rivers flow on every continent and on all but the smallest island. They occur with an almost bewildering variety, ranging from a mere trickle to a mighty surge. As a source of water, rivers have always been objects of wonder and practical concern for people everywhere. They have acted as cradles for civilization and agents of disaster. A river may be a barrier or a highway. It can bear trade and sediment; culture and conflict. A river may inspire or it may terrify.

This book shines a light on the numerous roles that rivers have played in the life of our planet and its inhabitants, highlighting their importance to facets both obvious and obscure, ranging from sanitation to ichthyology, via divinity and literary criticism. The flow of rivers has inspired poets and painters, philosophers and scientists, explorers and pilgrims. No one can hope to understand the city of London without an appreciation of the River Thames, nor Egypt without the Nile. Rivers have lent their names to countries and determined the outcomes of wars.

A river can cleave a deep canyon and twist like a giant snake across its plains; plunge over great cliffs and stretch fingers of earth into the oceans. Rivers dominate landscapes, eroding and creating them. They are, without doubt, the product of a complex suite of natural processes. But the evolution of many rivers has been driven as much by social systems as by natural ones, surprising though this may at first seem.

Physically, people have long interacted with rivers, extracting their water and fish, modifying them to suit their needs. Rivers, in turn, have influenced innumerable aspects of culture through the ages, generating both myths and hydro-energy. Rivers have their place in legend, religion, and many other aspects of society, including music, art, and poetry. They are, therefore, not simply physical objects, part of the material world, but also cultural entities which interact with the social system. In many ways, rivers convey values as much as water.

It may not be surprising, then, to learn that precisely defining a river is not an easy task. Our friend the *Oxford English Dictionary* has it that a river is 'a copious natural stream of water flowing in a channel to the sea or a lake etc'. This definition serves for many rivers but not for all. Rivers in very cold places do not flow all the time. Neither do most rivers in deserts. In the former case, the water is frozen for lengthy periods; in the latter, there is often no water at all. The word 'copious' is tricky, too. Many readers will make a distinction in their minds between a river and a smaller body of water, such as a brook or stream. However, not all do. In legal terms, the word 'river' usually includes all natural streams, no matter how small. More difficult still is the word 'natural'. People have been interacting with rivers and changing them for thousands of years, so that today there are not many that can be described as completely natural and unmodified. To complete our deconstruction of the dictionary definition, let us remember that not all rivers flow into the sea or a lake. Some rivers disappear into the ground or dry up completely before reaching another body of water.

So, contrary to what we expect of a dictionary, its definition is not universal. This is not a modern conundrum. Dr James Clyde, whose book *Elementary Geography* reached its 25th edition in the late 19th century, was presented with it in his article on 'Rivers

1. Rivers play a primary role in shaping landscapes, sometimes in dramatic ways, as here in the Himalayan mountains in Nepal

and Rivers' in the *Scottish Geographical Journal* of 1885. He ducked the issue by paraphrasing John Stuart Mill in renouncing the metaphysical nicety of definition: 'every one has a notion, sufficiently correct for common purposes, of what is meant by river'.

There is a body of geographical research into how small children perceive their surroundings, and their notions of what a river should be are as good as any. Some of the best taken from a recent study are: 'wet water running down', 'a long blue thing that's wet', and 'something that flows and has fish and water'. All are sufficiently correct for our purposes.

Chapter 1
Nature's driver

Water is the driver of Nature.

Leonardo da Vinci (1452–1519)
(Italian painter, architect, and engineer)

We live on a wet planet. Water is the most abundant substance on Earth and covers two-thirds of its surface. It is also found in smaller quantities in the air we breathe, the plants and animals we see, and the ground on which we tread. This water is continuously on the move, being recycled between the land, oceans, and atmosphere: an eternal succession known as the hydrological cycle. Rivers play a key role in the hydrological cycle, draining water from the land and moving it ultimately to the sea.

Any rain or melted snow that doesn't evaporate or seep into the earth flows downhill over the land surface under the influence of gravity. This flow is channelled by small irregularities in the topography into rivulets that merge to become gullies that feed into larger channels. The flow of rivers is augmented with water flowing through the soil and from underground stores, but a river is more than simply water flowing to the sea. A river also carries rocks and other sediments, dissolved minerals, plants, and animals, both dead and alive. In doing so, rivers transport large amounts of material and provide habitats for a great variety of wildlife. They carve valleys and deposit plains, being largely responsible for shaping the Earth's continental landscapes.

Rivers change progressively over their course from headwaters to mouth, from steep streams that are narrow and turbulent to wider, deeper, often meandering channels. From upstream to downstream, a continuum of change occurs: the volume of water flowing usually increases and coarse sediments grade into finer material. In its upper reaches, a river erodes its bed and banks, but this removal of earth, pebbles, and sometimes boulders gives way to the deposition of material in lower reaches. In tune with these variations in the physical characteristics of the river, changes can also be seen in the types of creatures and plants that make the river their home.

Its narrow, linear form and its flow in just one direction provide an obvious spatial dimension to how we should describe and understand the physical, chemical, and biological properties of a river: horizontally from upstream to downstream. But a river is not just a channel. It is also an integral part of the countryside through which it flows, so a lateral dimension, to the surrounding landscape, is also appropriate. The links with the landscape, or riverscape as some would prefer, are innumerable. They range from the simple fact that most water in a river arrives in the channel after flowing across the surrounding topography to the importance of salmon in a river, say, as a seasonal source of food for local bears.

A third dimension is vertical. Rivers interact with the sediments beneath the channel and with the air above. The water flowing in many rivers comes both directly from the air as rainfall – or another form of precipitation – and also from groundwater sources held in rocks and gravels beneath, both being flows of water through the hydrological cycle.

The vital fourth dimension, time, also has an important place in river research. This is because of profound variations in many factors that affect rivers, not least the amount of water flowing in them. This varies on a wide range of timescales, from an intense rainstorm that lasts less than an hour to the effects of tectonic forces that operate over many millions of years.

Rivers are found all over the world and have left their mark on virtually every landscape. Certain areas lack surface drainage, but in some of these regions rivers flow beneath the land surface. In deserts, many rivers remain dry for most of the year, only channelling water in response to a sporadic rainstorm. Elsewhere, fossil channels and valleys indicate where rivers have flowed at some time in the more distant past. Such fossilized features also occur on other planets: channels and valleys have been identified on Mars and on Titan – the largest of Saturn's moons – and these networks are remarkably similar to river and stream features on Earth. On the surface of Mars, these features have been sculpted by flowing water in times past, but the river channels and drainage networks on Titan are thought to have been formed by the flow of liquid methane. For most of our planet's land surface, a flowing river of water is one of the most fundamental elements. Supplied with energy from sunlight and gravity, it is a feature that moulds valleys and slopes and provides a complex habitat for living communities.

River hierarchies

One interesting aspect of rivers is that they seem to be organized hierarchically. When viewed from an aircraft or on a map, rivers form distinct networks like the branches of a tree. Small tributary channels join together to form larger channels which in turn merge to form still larger rivers. This progressive increase in river size is often described using a numerical ordering scheme in which the smallest stream is called first order, the union of two first-order channels produces a second-order river, the union of two second-order channels produces a third-order river, and so on. Stream order only increases when two channels of the same rank merge. Very large rivers, such as the Nile and Mississippi, are tenth-order rivers; the Amazon twelfth order.

Each river drains an area of land that is proportional to its size. This area is known by several different terms: drainage basin, river basin, or catchment ('watershed' is also used in American English, but this word means the drainage divide between two adjacent basins in British English). In the same way that a river network is made up of a hierarchy of low-order rivers nested within higher-order rivers, their drainage basins also fit together to form a nested hierarchy. In other words, smaller units are repeating elements nested within larger units. All of these units are linked by flows of water, sediment, and energy.

Recognizing rivers as being made up of a series of units that are arranged hierarchically provides a potent framework in which to study the patterns and processes associated with rivers. At the largest scale, the entire river basin can be studied. Within the basin, at progressively smaller scales, a researcher may focus on a particular segment of a river between tributaries, a reach within a segment, and so on all the way down to a small patch of sand grains on the river bed. This hierarchical approach also emphasizes that processes operating at the upper levels of the hierarchy exert considerable influence over features lower down in the hierarchy, but not the other way around. At the river basin scale, important factors are climate, geology, vegetation, and topography. These factors have an influence at all lesser scales, down to the small patch of sand grains. That patch of sand also comes under other local influences, such as ripples in the flowing water, but these small variations in the current have a negligible impact on the drainage basin as a whole.

There is an appropriate timescale associated with related spatial scales and these too can be arranged into a hierarchy. Generally, the larger the spatial scale, the slower the processes and rates of change. Changes in climate and geology, for instance, occur on lengthy timescales, such as hundreds to millions of years. The ripples in the water operate on much shorter timescales: milliseconds to seconds.

It is also important to remember that, in general terms, as size increases, so too does the complexity of factors influencing the landscape and the river running through it. Hence, the small catchment of a first-order river channel, for example, may well occur on one rock type and lie within one climatic region. A larger catchment is more likely to span several rock types and climatic regions and is therefore more complex.

Types of river

The numerical ordering scheme detailed in the previous section is one of many attempts to classify rivers. There is an enormous variety of different types of river, or 'fluvial' system (from the Latin word *fluvius*, a river), when we extend our area of interest beyond the river channel to include the entire drainage basin. Each river classification depends on the perspective of the investigator and hence the aspect of greatest significance. A biologist may focus on the distribution of particular groups of organisms such as fish or aquatic plants. Different species may be associated with different types of topography and geology, for example, hence rivers may be placed in categories such as 'mountainous', 'upland', 'lowland chalk', 'lowland sandstone', and 'lowland and upland clay'. Others have used selected chemical factors as a basis for classification. An example is pH, so rivers might be classed as being strongly acid, slightly acid, or alkaline. An authority concerned with nature conservation might combine all of these perspectives and more. A classification of rivers in England, Wales, and Scotland based on vegetation communities devised by the Nature Conservancy Council recognizes four main groups of rivers, ten types, and thirty-eight sub-types.

Another simple way of categorizing rivers is by size. Some authorities prefer the word 'stream' when referring to rivers at one end of the size spectrum. A large or big river (both words are in common use to signify the other end of the spectrum) is usually one with either a large drainage basin, a long course, one that transports a large volume of sediment, or has a great volume of water flowing in it. We have noted that there is a consistent relationship between river length and drainage basin area, although not between the other variables due to variations in basin geology, relief, and hydrology. Most people when asked to list the world's largest rivers would come up with a similar list for their top 10 or 20, but a perfect definition remains elusive.

The pattern formed in a landscape by a network of rivers is a familiar way of distinguishing between different types of river system. There are several common variations on the essentially treelike pattern of a drainage network, and various descriptive terms are used, including dendritic, radial, trellis, parallel, and rectangular. The primary influence on these patterns is the geology of the landscape.

2. This satellite image of the Central Siberian Plateau illustrates a typical drainage network. Snow at higher altitudes contrasts with the snow-free valleys, helping to accentuate the drainage pattern

An obvious way of categorizing different types of river is by their types of flow. A river channel that carries water at all times throughout the year is described as 'perennial', but this does not describe all rivers by any means. Some channels have water flowing in them only in particular seasons. These seasonal, or 'intermittent', rivers may be in regions with a severe winter in which river water completely freezes, or in regions with a distinct wet season. A river with an even less permanent flow of water is described as 'ephemeral' and consists of channels that flow only for hours or days following individual rainstorms. Rivers that arise and flow in deserts are typically ephemeral rivers. A fourth category is the 'interrupted' river, one that has permanent flow over short reaches throughout the year while most of the river is dry. While these distinctions are undoubtedly real, like most classification schemes in the natural world, the boundaries between different classes are better viewed as points on a continuum of flow regime types. This is because, for example, during an extended wet period lasting several years, an ephemeral river may exhibit the characteristics of a seasonal river, while during dry periods, the wet season flow of a seasonal river may be absent or more intermittent, making it appear more like an ephemeral river.

How long is a river?

Measuring the length of a river is more complicated than it sounds. Measurements and estimates for the length of the world's rivers vary greatly depending on all sorts of factors, including the season of the year, the abilities of the cartographer, and the quality of his equipment, as well as decisions about what exactly is measured. In theory, the exercise should be straightforward: determine the position of the source, identify the mouth, and accurately measure the length of the river between the two. Finding the mouth is usually clear-cut. Its exact location is commonly defined as the intersection between the central line of the river and a line drawn between the two sides of the outlet.

Determining the exact location of the source is often more difficult. Searches for the source of particular rivers in remote and inaccessible regions have intrigued and inspired explorers for centuries, and continue to do so even today.

Disagreements about the true source of many rivers have been a continuous feature of this history of exploration. In one sense, a mission to find 'the' source of a river is destined to be a matter of conjecture simply because most rivers typically have many tributaries and hence numerous sources. For most authorities, the source that is farthest away from the mouth is considered to be 'the' source of the river, thus giving a maximum river length. But, unsurprisingly, differences arise as to the farthest source.

Another complicating factor is whether or not to include tributaries that have been given different names. In practice, the series of decisions made about the inclusion or exclusion of tributaries is probably the major element of a quest to find the source of a river, and these decisions represent one of the central reasons why not all measurements for a particular river agree. Take the Mekong as an example. Everyone acknowledges that the river originates on the Tibetan Plateau, but where exactly is open to debate. Candidates for its source include glaciers on the Guozongmucha Mountain, Lasaigongma Mountain, Zhanarigen Mountain, Chajiarima Mountain, and Mount Jifu. Others include Rup-sa La Pass, Lungmo Pass, and Lake Zhaxiqiwa. Given the number of designated sources, perhaps it is not surprising that the Mekong is variously referred to as the ninth longest and the twelfth longest river in the world, and that is without going into similar confusion surrounding many of the other major world rivers. Respectable texts give the length of the Mekong as anything between 4,180 kilometres and 4,909 kilometres. If we accept that the river's source is on Mount Jifu, which many do not, the river has six names along its 4,909-kilometre length. On the flanks of Mount Jifu, melted snow and ice flow as a stream named the Guyong-Pudigao Creek (which only flows in the summer). After just over 20 kilometres, this becomes the Guoyong River, which becomes the Zhaa River. The Zhaa merges with the Zhana River to become the Zha River, which becomes the Lancang River until it reaches the Chinese border with Myanmar, where it is known as the Mekong all the way to its delta in southern Vietnam. In its delta, the river splits into several branches that flow into the South China Sea.

Some say this is the Mekong in its entirety, and that it is 4,909 kilometres long. Others agree that it is 4,909 kilometres long but say that strictly the river should be called the Mekong- Lancang-Zha-Zhaa-Guoyong-Guyong-Pudigao. Another group would prefer to deal only with the stretch that carries the name Mekong, in which case the river is actually just 2,711 kilometres long. Many others differ more profoundly because for them the source is not on Mount Jifu at all.

If you are bemused, it is understandable. But it gets more confusing. Some rivers do not have a mouth. The Okavango River in southern Africa gradually diminishes into the inland Okavango delta, the size of which varies with the seasons. Hence, the exact point where the river ends changes seasonally. Some rivers have more than one channel. The length of which channel should be measured in a 'braided' (see below) stretch of river? The timing of measurement is also important. Guyong-Pudigao Creek on Mount Jifu only has water flowing in it during the summer melt season. Should it be counted if the flow is not continuous? Another difficulty of timing occurs in rivers that flood seasonally. When large stretches of the Amazon, for example, flood in the wet season, water that flows round a meander in the dry season flows more directly 'overland'. Should the length of the meander be counted, or not? Over longer periods of time, rivers can create new land, by depositing sediment in deltas, for example, so increasing their length.

Yet another important part of measuring the length of a river is the scale at which it is measured. Fundamentally, the length of a river varies with the map scale because different amounts of detail are generalized at different scales. The terrain along the course of a river has great complexity, with details nested within details. This geometric complexity, a quality known as 'fractal' that is inherent in many natural things, can be taken to the absurd. But when does a desire for greater detail cross the boundary into the realms of the absurd?

The use of satellite mapping, along with Global Positioning Systems (GPS), to establish accurate source locations will continue to improve our ability to study river systems in their entirety, but subjective decisions about the scale of study and which tributaries to include and exclude will continue to mean that it is effectively impossible to say definitively which river holds the 'world's longest' title. The Amazon and the Nile have been the main contenders for centuries as knowledge has improved and conventions have changed. The Scottish explorer John Hanning Speke thought he had solved one of the great mysteries of 19th-century world geography when he claimed in 1858 to have discovered that the source of the Nile was Lake Victoria. For much of the 20th century, most authorities recognized the Nile as the world's longest river, having added the longest tributary leading into Lake Victoria from the south. However, since the 1990s several credible claims have been made for the Amazon to be longer, following a number of expeditions in search of its source in the mountains of southern Peru. These claims put the length of the Amazon at some 6,850 kilometres, at least 150 kilometres longer than the Nile, but the debate is unlikely to end there.

River flow

Two particularly important properties of river flow are velocity and discharge – the volume of water moving past a point over some interval of time, although confusingly this may also be called simply the flow. A continuous record of discharge plotted against time is called a hydrograph which, depending on the time frame

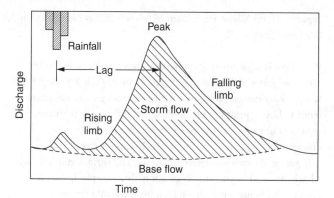

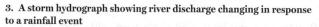

3. A storm hydrograph showing river discharge changing in response to a rainfall event

chosen, may give a detailed depiction of a flood event over a few days, or the discharge pattern over a year or more.

Measuring the flow of rivers and analysing the records is important for evaluating water resources and the assessment of flood and drought hazards. No river has a longer hydrological record than the Nile, where a water-level gauging structure was built on Roda Island at Cairo in AD 641. The official in charge of the Roda 'nilometer', the Sheikh el Mikyas, had the duty of observing the water level and during times of flood announcing the daily rise via public criers. This was always a tense time of year in Egypt. If the river did not reach a certain level, much cropland would go without water and famine could be expected, but at a certain higher level irrigation was assured, and with it taxes to the government. The position of Sheikh el Mikyas continued for more than 1,000 years. The last holder of the post died in 1947, and in the 1950s the Egyptian government decided to construct a major dam on the Nile at Aswan, thus significantly changing the country's intimate relationship with its river. The record from the Roda nilometer was invaluable in calculating the required storage capacity of the Aswan High Dam which was finally completed in 1970 (see Chapter 5).

River flow is dependent upon many different factors, including the area and shape of the drainage basin. If all else is equal, larger basins experience larger flows. A river draining a circular basin tends to have a peak in flow because water from all its tributaries arrives at more or less the same time as compared to a river draining a long, narrow basin in which water arrives from tributaries in a more staggered manner. The surface conditions in a basin are also important. Vegetation, for example, intercepts rainfall and hence slows down its movement into rivers.

Climate is a particularly significant determinant of river flow. It is the major factor controlling the different types of flow identified above: perennial, intermittent, ephemeral, and interrupted. All the rivers with the greatest flows are almost entirely located in the humid tropics, where rainfall is abundant throughout the year. These are the Amazon, the Congo, and the Orinoco, each of which discharges more than 1,000 cubic kilometres of water into the oceans in an average year.

Rivers in the humid tropics experience relatively constant flows throughout the year, but perennial rivers in more seasonal climates exhibit marked seasonality in flow. The Indus River receives most of its water from the Himalayan mountains and the maximum summer discharge is over 100 times the winter minimum due to the effect of snowmelt. Minimum discharge is often zero in rivers flowing largely in areas of high latitude and high altitude, where temperatures fall below freezing point for a portion of the year. In these intermittent rivers, the distinct contrast between minimum flow during the frozen winter and great floods during the summer melt season is regular and predictable.

By contrast, the flow of ephemeral rivers, typically found in desert areas, is spasmodic and unpredictable. This is because ephemeral rivers respond to rainfall which is notoriously difficult to predict in many deserts. One study of a river bed in the northern Negev Desert in Israel showed that on average the channel contained water for just 2% of the time, or about seven days a year. Some desert rivers can go for an entire year without any flow.

Year-to-year variations in river flow are also greatest in dry climates, whereas perennial rivers in the humid tropics have relatively steady flows from one year to the next. Records of discharge in the middle reaches of the Kuiseb River in the Namib Desert in Namibia over several decades show that flow has varied from 0 to 102 days per year.

Over longer periods, changes in rainfall and temperature have also resulted in changes in river flow regimes, although human interference has confused the picture in many cases (see Chapter 5). One of the clearest recent changes in natural flows is in West Africa where the desert-marginal belt to the south of the Sahara known as the Sahel experienced a marked desiccation of the climate over the last few decades of the 20th century, a trend that has continued into the 21st century. The flow of the Senegal River measured at Bakel, near the meeting of the borders between Senegal, Mauritania, and Mali, showed a marked decline towards the end of the last century. The average annual discharge at Bakel for the period 1904–92 was 716 cubic metres per second, but that average was just 379 cubic metres per second over the period 1972–92. The flow in 1984, a particularly dry year, averaged out at 212 cubic metres per second. A similar picture has been seen on the Niger River.

Some rivers are large enough to flow through more than one climate region. Some desert rivers, for instance, are perennial because they receive most of their flow from high rainfall areas outside the desert. These are known as 'exotic' rivers. The Nile is an example, as is the Murray in Australia. These rivers lose large amounts of water – by evaporation and infiltration into soils – while flowing through the desert, but their volumes are such that they maintain their continuity and reach the sea. By contrast, many exotic desert rivers do not flow into the sea but deliver their water to interior basins. In southern Africa, water from the tropical highlands in Angola flows in the Okavango River to the Okavango Delta, the large wetland area in the Kalahari Desert in northern Botswana. In central Asia, water from the Parmir Mountains flows into the Aral Sea via two of central Asia's major exotic rivers: the Syr Darya and Amu Darya.

Some rivers are thought to be very old. Evidence from sediments deposited near the mouth of the Amazon suggests that the river has been flowing across South America for 11 million years. Over such great periods of time, all sorts of factors change, of course, and some rivers come and go. An example of a river that has disappeared is the Channel River which flowed westward in northwestern Europe some 20,000 years ago in the area now submerged beneath the English Channel separating Britain and France. This was the height of the last Ice Age, when sea levels all over the world were much lower than they are today because more water in the hydrological cycle was present as ice. Most of the British Isles and all of Scandinavia were covered in a thick ice sheet at this time, and the Channel River was fed by meltwater that flowed in the rivers of southern England, including the Thames and the Solent, that lay just beyond the permanent ice. Among the Channel River's other tributaries to the south were the Seine, Somme, Maas, Rhine, and Elbe.

Such ancient river channels are not solely of academic interest. The world's richest gold deposits, in the Witwatersrand district of South Africa, were laid down in river systems more than two billion years ago. Gold carried by these rivers was deposited in gravels where the velocity of the flowing water slowed. These gravels, known to geologists as Witwatersrand conglomerate, have produced nearly 50,000 tonnes, or 40%, of the gold ever mined, and probably still contain over one-third of the world's unmined gold reserves. Rivers have also played a key role in creating the valuable diamond deposits that stretch along the western coast of southern Africa. Diamonds have been eroded from deposits inland and carried to the coastline by the Vaal and Orange Rivers for 100 million years and more. This fluvial transport is also thought to be beneficial to the quality of the diamonds found in coastal sediments because the stones tend to break down during transport, increasing the concentration of higher-quality diamonds.

Erosion, transport, and deposition

An important measure of the way a river system moulds its landscape is the 'drainage density'. This is the sum of the channel length divided by the total area drained, which reflects the spacing of channels. Hence, drainage density expresses the degree to which a river dissects the landscape, effectively controlling the texture of relief. Numerous studies have shown that drainage density has a great range in different regions, depending on conditions of climate, vegetation, and geology particularly. The value tends to be high in arid regions of sparse vegetation, in temperate to tropical regions subjected to frequent heavy rains, and in areas underlain by rocks that are difficult for water to penetrate.

Rivers shape the Earth's continental landscapes in three main ways: by the erosion, transport, and deposition of sediments. These three processes have been used to recognize a simple three-part classification of individual rivers and river networks according to the dominant process in each of three areas: source, transfer, and depositional zones.

The first zone consists of the river's upper reaches, the area from which most of the water and sediment are derived. This is where most of the river's erosion occurs, and this eroded material is transported through the second zone to be deposited in the third zone. These three zones are idealized because some sediment is eroded, stored, and transported in each of them, but within each zone one process is dominant.

The changes in a river's slope that occur between its upper and lower reaches are reflected in a graphical measurement known as the 'long profile'. This is a section through the channel from its headwater to its mouth and is typically concave in shape because the headwaters are steep and slope decreases progressively in a downstream direction. This generally smooth, concave-upwards form is sometimes interrupted by outcrops of hard rocks that produce locally steeper slopes. Rapids form in these areas and the velocity of the river increases, promoting greater erosion, which over a long time period wears down the obstruction. In a place where relatively soft rocks are overlain by much more resistant rocks, a waterfall may occur. The world's highest waterfall, Angel Falls, or Kerepakupai Merú, cascades over a very hard sandstone rockface in Venezuela and is an awe-inspiring 979 metres in height.

All of the sediment carried by a river ultimately comes from the erosion of surrounding slopes and water flowing across and through the land surface, but the immediate supply comes from the bed and banks of the river channel. The flow of water carries this sediment in three ways: dissolved material – such as calcium, magnesium, and other minerals – moves in solution; small particles are carried in suspension; and larger particles are transported along the stream bed by rolling, sliding, or a bouncing movement known as 'saltation'. This material is deposited when circumstances change in some way, such as the slope of the river bed decreasing, so reducing the river's energy and ability to carry its load. Much of it is deposited in the sea. Globally, it is estimated that rivers transport around 15 billion tonnes of suspended material annually to the oceans, plus about another 4 billion tonnes of dissolved material.

In its upper reaches, a river might flow across bedrock but further downstream this is much less likely. Alluvial rivers are flanked by a floodplain, the channel cut into material that the river itself has transported and deposited. The floodplain is a relatively flat area which is periodically inundated during periods of high flow, typically every one or two years. When water spills out onto the floodplain, the velocity of flow decreases and sediment begins to settle, causing fresh deposits of alluvium on the floodplain.

Certain patterns of alluvial river channels have been seen on every continent and are divided at the most basic level into straight, meandering, and braided. Straight channels are rare in nature and, for the most part, are a function of the scale of assessment. They are described as straight at the regional scale, but at more local scales they are winding or sinuous to some degree. The most common river channel pattern is a series of bends known as meanders, named after the River Menderes in southwestern Turkey, which is well known for its sinuosity. Meanders develop because erosion becomes concentrated on the outside of a bend and deposition on the inside. As these linked processes continue, the meander bend can become more emphasized, and a particularly sinuous meander may eventually be cut off at its narrow neck, leaving an oxbow lake as evidence of its former course. Alluvial meanders migrate, both down and across their floodplain, a process that can be monitored by comparing old maps and repeated photography. This lateral migration is an important process in the formation of floodplains.

Braided rivers can be recognized by their numerous flows that split off and rejoin each other to give a braided appearance. These multiple intersecting flows are separated by small and often temporary islands of alluvium. Braided rivers typically carry abundant sediment and are found in areas with a fairly steep gradient, often near mountainous regions. The reason why one channel meanders and another is braided has been the subject of considerable research. Important factors that influence the channel pattern include the volume of water and velocity of flow, which are related in turn to the gradient of the channel and the

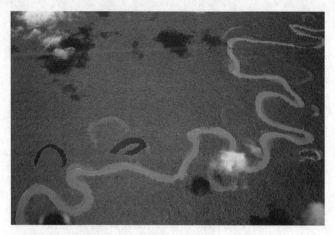

4. A meandering river and oxbow lakes in a remote part of New Guinea

nature of the channel, particularly the ease with which its bed and bank is eroded, which affects the supply of sediment to the river. These factors can change, over time and through space. For example, the Milk River in North America is a classic meandering river as it flows across southern Alberta in Canada but changes abruptly to a braided pattern shortly after entering Montana, USA. The change is probably due to differences in the material that makes up the bed and banks and a widening of the channel in the braided reach which reduces the power of the river.

The meander cut-off creating an oxbow lake is one way in which a channel makes an abrupt change of course, a characteristic of some alluvial rivers that is generally referred to as 'avulsion'. It is a natural process by which flow diverts out of an established channel into a new permanent course on the adjacent floodplain, a change in course that can present a major threat to human activities. Rapid, frequent, and often significant avulsions have typified many rivers on the Indo-Gangetic plains of South Asia. In

India, the Kosi River has migrated about 100 kilometres westward in the last 200 years, and the Gandak River has moved about 80 kilometres to the east over the last 5,000 years. The lower Indus River in Pakistan also has a history of major avulsions. Why a river suddenly avulses is not understood completely, but earthquakes play a part on the Indo-Gangetic plains.

Sometimes an avulsion can result in a channel being left dry, but on other occasions the channel becomes split, creating a river that flows in multiple channels. These multi-channel rivers are called 'anastomosing' or 'anabranching' rivers. At first sight, an anastomosing river can easily be confused with a braided river, which has a roughly comparable pattern. A braided river has multiple flows within a single channel, whereas an anastomosing river has multiple interconnected channels. Nonetheless, debates about the differences continue and numerous classifications of channel pattern are used. Misunderstandings can also arise when river flow is high or low. At high discharge, a braided river with submerged bars may look like a single-thread channel, and at low discharge an anastomosing river may carry water in a single main channel only, so appearing as a single-channel river.

Most rivers eventually flow into the sea or a lake, where they deposit sediment which builds up into a landform known as a delta. The name comes from the Greek letter delta, Δ, shaped like a triangle or fan, one of the classic shapes a delta can take. Examples of this type of delta include two of Africa's largest: those at the conclusion of the Niger and Nile Rivers.

The river provides the sediment that makes up a delta, but there are many other influences on its shape, including the volume of water flowing, the amount of sediment, and the relative importance of the flow of the river, the ebb and flow of tides, and the energy of waves. Fan-shaped deltas like the Niger and Nile are dominated by the action of the waves. Deltas dominated by the flow of the river typically extend further out into the sea as a lobe,

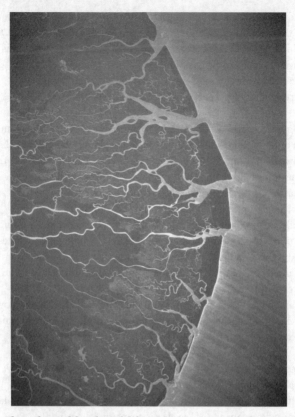

5. The archetypal fan-shaped delta of the Niger River, the largest delta in Africa

its channels branching like the toes or claws of a bird. The Mississippi River delta is an example of the 'bird-foot delta' type. Tide-dominated deltas form in locations with a large tidal range or fast tidal currents. They are typified by numerous islands elongated parallel to the main tidal flow and perpendicular to the shore line. Good examples are the deltas of the Fly River in New Guinea and the delta at the confluence of the Brahmaputra and Ganges Rivers.

Material laid down at the end of a river can continue underwater far beyond the delta as a deep-sea fan. The world's largest submarine fan lies beyond the Ganges-Brahmaputra delta. The Bengal Deep-Sea Fan is almost 3,000 kilometres long, more than 1,000 kilometres wide, and may be more than 16 kilometres thick at its deepest part. It is linked to the Ganges-Brahmaputra delta by a submarine canyon which funnels the sediment from the river to the deep-sea bed. The origins of the fan date from the collision of India with Eurasia, the tectonic event that created the Himalayan mountain range, making it more than 40 million years old.

River ecology

A great diversity of creatures makes up the ecology of rivers, an interconnected web of life that ranges from microscopic algae to huge fish larger than a human being. Their diverse communities reflect the great array of running water environments that vary from large lowland rivers occupying basins on a subcontinental scale to small, turbulent mountain brooks. The physical structure of the river is one set of influences on its ecology, but chemical and biological attributes are also important, and all are to some degree related. The water's oxygen content, acidity or alkalinity, nutrients, metals, and other constituents are all determined largely by the types of soil and rock that make up the drainage basin, but also in part by interactions with plants and animals both in the water and on land.

The organisms found in fluvial ecosystems are commonly classified according to the methods they use to gather food and feed. 'Shredders' are organisms that consume small sections of leaves; 'grazers' and 'scrapers' consume algae from the surfaces of objects such as stones and large plants; 'collectors' feed on fine organic matter produced by the breakdown of other once-living things; and 'predators' eat other living creatures. The relative importance of these groups of creatures typically changes as one moves from the headwaters of a river to stretches further downstream, reflecting physical factors such as channel width, shading by trees, and the velocity of the water. This is the 'river continuum concept' which describes a continuum of changes that integrate energy sources, food webs, and stream order in an essentially linear way. Hence, small headwater streams are often shaded by overhanging vegetation which limits sunlight and photosynthesis but contributes organic matter by leaf fall. Shredders and collectors typically dominate in these stretches, but further downstream, where the river is wider and thus receives more sunlight and less leaf fall, the situation is quite different. Here, food chains are typically based on living plant material rather than leaf fall, so there are few shredders and probably more predators.

The river continuum concept is a popular model that has influenced many studies of fluvial ecosystems, but it is not the only one. Another important model used to study river ecology stresses the importance of the annual pulse of floodwaters that extends many rivers in temperate and tropical regions on to their floodplains. The 'flood-pulse concept' broadens the focus beyond the main river channel and puts much greater emphasis on interactions with a greater variety of habitats such as the marshes and lakes typically found on floodplains. These habitats are broadly synonymous with the river's 'riparian' zone (from the Latin word *ripa*, a bank), made up of any land that adjoins, regularly influences, or is influenced by a body of water. Vegetation in the riparian zone helps to maintain the condition of aquatic ecosystems in several ways. These include providing bank stability and so minimizing erosion, filtering sediment, and processing nutrients from the drainage basin, particularly nitrogen. Fallen branches or trunks from riparian trees also create woody habitat areas for many fish and smaller creatures.

From the ecological perspective, the unidirectional flow of a river is a unique situation. Flowing water influences many aspects of the river environment, moving things and thus helping to disperse organisms and transport nutrients. Flowing water affects the shape of the channel and the nature of its bed, disturbing both on occasions of strong flow, maintaining a dynamic habitat for fluvial plants and animals. Rivers also deliver water, energy, sediment, and organic matter to marine ecosystems. This flow is overwhelmingly in one direction, but not entirely so. Some fish swim against the flow, migrating upstream to spawn, for instance. Fish that migrate from the sea into fresh water for breeding, so-called 'anadromous' species, such as salmon, are prime examples. Salmon attain most of their body mass feeding at sea, so when they die in a river after spawning their carcasses make an important contribution of nutrients and energy to both aquatic and adjacent terrestrial ecosystems.

The flow of water has almost inevitably produced an emphasis on spatial complexity in studies of river ecology, but variations in stream flow over time are also important. The quantity, timing, and variability of a river's flow create a mosaic of habitats to which fluvial organisms have adapted. The ecology of rivers in regions with a Mediterranean climate, for example, is attuned to substantial seasonal variability in flow because most of the rain falls in winter (often 80% or more in three months). A cool, wet season is followed by a warm, dry season which produces a rhythm of flooding and drying in the rivers, although the intensity of each season can vary markedly from year to year.

There's no doubting the numerous fundamental ways in which a river's biology is dependent upon its physical setting, particularly in terms of climate, geology, and topography. Nevertheless, these relationships also work in reverse. The biological components of rivers also act to shape the physical environment, particularly at more local scales. Beavers provide a good illustration of the ways in which the physical structure of rivers can be changed profoundly by large mammals. They cut wood and construct dams, trapping sediments and organic material, modifying nutrient cycles, and ultimately influencing many other communities of plants and animals.

Finally, it is worth emphasizing again the many ways in which the ecology of rivers has effects far beyond the channel itself. In the same way that a river plays a key role in shaping the landscape it moves through, its flow provides important services to many of the plants and animals that inhabit that terrain. The most obvious of these is as a source of water and sustenance. Flowing water both delivers and removes many vital nutrients and other constituents to and from ecosystems, but rivers also have effects that may be less immediately obvious. The distribution of many terrestrial plant and animal species concords with the geography of major river systems because rivers can act both as corridors for species dispersal but also as barriers to the dispersal of organisms. One of the first to recognize the importance of rivers as obstacles to the movement of certain creatures was the naturalist Alfred Russel Wallace, who in the mid-19th century defined distinct areas in South America bounded by major rivers in the Amazon Basin, each with its own distinct communities of species. This idea of the river acting as a barrier is one of a number of hypotheses put forward to explain the evolutionary origin of the astonishing richness of species found in Amazonian forests.

The Amazon: mightiest of them all

By almost every measure, the Amazon is the greatest of all the large rivers. Encompassing more than 7 million square kilometres, its drainage basin is the largest in the world and makes up 5% of the global land surface. The river accounts for nearly one-fifth of all the river water discharged into the oceans. The flow is so great that water from the Amazon can still be identified 125 miles out in the Atlantic: early sailors could drink fresh water from the ocean long before their first sighting of the South American continent. Nonetheless, the lower reaches of the Amazon flow down such a gentle gradient that the physical influence of sea tides can still be identified more than 1,000 kilometres upstream from the Atlantic.

The Amazon has some 1,100 tributaries, and 7 of these are more than 1,600 kilometres long. The main tributaries are often classified according to the colour of their waters, which also reflects their source. Black-water tributaries attain their tea colour from high levels of dissolved plant matter leached from low-lying areas of sandy soils. White-water rivers are coloured by the high loads of sediments transported from the Andes. The clear-water rivers carry low levels of sediments and organic matter from the crystalline rocks of the Guyana and Brazilian shields.

In the lowlands, most Amazonian rivers have extensive floodplains studded with thousands of shallow lakes. Up to one-quarter of the entire Amazon Basin is periodically flooded, and these lakes become progressively connected with each other as the water level rises. Researchers using GPS have measured a sizeable part of South America sinking by nearly 8 centimetres because of the extra weight due to flooding in the Amazon, an area that rises again as the waters recede. This annual rise and fall of the Earth's crust is the largest we have detected.

Many of the Amazon's plants and animals have adapted to living in an environment that is seasonally waterlogged, some areas for up to 11 months a year and to depths of 13 metres. Many tree species of the Amazon rainforest depend on the floods for seed dispersal, for example, either floating downriver or through fish species that are dependent on fruits and seeds. The great diversity of the Amazon's aquatic habitats has played a key role in producing the most diverse fish fauna on the planet. In total, with about 2,500 fish species that have been described by scientists (and probably more than 1,000 still awaiting description), the Amazon's species richness comfortably exceeds that of all other large river basins. Its two mightiest fish, the arapaima and the piraíba, each has a maximum weight of about 200 kilograms, more than twice that of an average man.

The one measure by which the Amazon is not generally regarded as the greatest of all rivers is length. It is comfortably the longest in the Americas, but most authorities place the Nile at the top of the world list. However, the difficulties in measuring the length of a river mean that debate on the matter will undoubtedly continue (see above).

The Onyx: an unusual river

The longest river in Antarctica, the River Onyx is just 32 kilometres in length and is in many respects quite different from rivers in most parts of the world. The Onyx is situated in the McMurdo Dry Valleys region, one of a small number of ice-free desert areas that occur along the coastline of an otherwise ice-covered continent. The climate is very dry and bitterly cold, with an average annual temperature of –20°C. The small amount of precipitation (less than 100 millimetres a year) that does fall comes only as dry snow and has virtually no direct effect on the river because fierce winds mean it never settles. Hence, the Onyx, and other rivers of the McMurdo Dry Valleys, flow for only four to ten weeks a year. This occurs during the summer when the temperature is warm enough to melt glacier ice, the only source of river water.

The Onyx flows from the Lower Wright Glacier into Lake Vanda, which has a salinity more than ten times that of seawater and a permanent cover of ice. There are no plants in the region and no fish or insects in the river, but worms, microscopic animals, and communities of algae growing as mats inhabit the river bed. These algal mats can survive long periods of desiccation, making the Onyx a relative hotspot of life in an otherwise barren landscape.

River floods

To hydrologists, the term 'flood' refers to a river's annual peak discharge period, whether the water inundates the surrounding landscape or not. In more common parlance, however, a flood is synonymous with the river overflowing its banks, and this is the meaning used here. Rivers flood in the normal course of events. This often occurs on the floodplain, as the name implies, but flooding can affect almost all of the length of a river.

Extreme weather, particularly heavy or prolonged rainfall, is the most frequent cause of flooding. The melting of snow and ice is another common cause. These events can often be predicted to an extent because they are seasonal. Other reasons for river floods are usually harder to anticipate. They include landslides, log jams, ice jams, avalanches, volcanic eruptions, and earthquakes.

River floods are one of the most common natural hazards affecting human society, frequently causing social disruption, material damage, and loss of life. Indeed, the largest ever death tolls from any natural hazards are attributed to flooding along the Yangtze and other Chinese rivers, with claims that some floods in the 20th century took the lives of millions of people: floods in 1931 and 1959 accounted for, respectively, 3.7 million and 2 million fatalities. It should be noted, however, that the death tolls reported for some floods in China vary a great deal, and other estimates for the 1931 and 1959 events put the death tolls much lower, in the hundreds of thousands. Hence, the statistics for some of these devastating floods, which are inevitably very difficult to calculate, should be treated with caution. Conversely, it is also worth noting that the scale of Chinese river flooding is astonishing and often undoubtedly affects hundreds of millions of people, as on the Yangtze in 1998, so the worst-case figures may not be so easy to dismiss.

The hazards associated with floods have encouraged the development of many techniques for predicting them. Flood hazard maps are commonly utilized for land-use zoning, enabling an authority to prohibit certain developments on land that is particularly flood-prone, for instance. Anticipating when a flood will occur can be done in several different ways. Most floods have a seasonal element in their occurrence and can often be forecast using meteorological observations, with the lag time to peak flow of a particular river in response to a rainstorm calculated using a flood hydrograph.

Other flood predictions seek to estimate the probable discharge which, on average, will be exceeded only once in any particular period, hence the use of such terms as '50-year flood' and '100-year flood'. It is a general rule that the magnitude of a flood is inversely related to its frequency, or probability, of occurrence (in other words, the larger the flood, the less likely it is). A flood that is likely to occur only once in a hundred years – the 100-year flood – has a 1% likelihood of occurring in any year, and the average interval between two floods of that magnitude is 100 years. For engineering purposes, it is useful to know the probability of a flood of a particular magnitude so that, for example, a bridge designed to last for 50 years can be built large enough to withstand a 50-year flood, and often a 100-year flood just in case. These are statistical probabilities, however, and there is still the chance that the bridge may be swept away by a far larger flood.

Many of the less predictable causes of flooding occur after a valley has been blocked by a natural dam as a result of a landslide, glacier, or lava flow. Natural dams may cause upstream flooding as the blocked river forms a lake and downstream flooding as a result of failure of the dam. Earthquakes, which can cause enormous landslides, are a particularly common cause of natural dams. For example, the Inangahua earthquake in South Island, New Zealand, in May 1968 triggered a huge landslide that dammed the Buller River. The rising water backed up for 7 kilometres, raising the river 30 metres above its normal level. Fears that the dam might suffer a catastrophic breach led to an evacuation of all the people living in its path, but the river eventually overflowed the landslide dam, eroding it downward gradually without causing serious flooding downstream.

Breaches of natural dams account for most of the largest known floods of the last 2.6 million years, the so-called Quaternary Period. The biggest that we know about occurred as a result of ice-dam failure after pre-existing continental drainage systems were blocked by ice sheets during the Ice Ages that have characterized the Quaternary. Some of the largest ever to have occurred on Earth were the Missoula floods in the northwestern USA of today. They resulted from the repeated breaching of an ice dam that blocked the present-day Clark Fork River between about 18,000 and 13,000 years ago. The ice created an immense lake known as glacial Lake Missoula which spilled out to create the Missoula floods when the ice dam periodically failed. The peak discharge of the Missoula floods is thought to have been a gigantic 17 million cubic metres per second, more than ten times the combined flow of all the rivers of the world today.

The evidence for the Missoula floods is convincing, but it is one of several great floods known or suspected to have occurred in prehistoric and geological times and not all are as well substantiated. Somewhere at the confluence of fact and fiction lie hundreds of flood legends from cultures all across the world. These stories take their place among a far greater number of myths, sacred traditions, and beliefs based on the flow of rivers that form the subject of the next chapter.

Chapter 2
Sacred flows

> Their Lord will guide them by their faith; there shall flow from
> beneath them rivers in gardens of bliss.

The Koran 10.9

Throughout history, the flow of rivers has nurtured life and spread
fertility to countless societies while also, on occasion, bringing
death and devastation. This dual function, as a force of nature that
sustains life but also takes it away, has generated cultural echoes
in groups all over the world. The powerful hold that rivers have
over humankind has become embedded in innumerable
traditions, myths, and sacred rituals through the ages.

Mythical rivers

In Greek mythology, the land of the dead, or underworld, was
surrounded by five rivers. These were the Acheron (the river of
woe), Cocytus (the river of lamentation), Phlegethon (the river of
fire), Lethe (the river of forgetfulness), and Styx (the river of hate).
When somebody died, the spirit of the dead was ferried across the
water (in some cases the Acheron, in others the Styx) by the
boatman, on payment of a fee. Each new arrival in the underworld
was judged, determined to be good or bad, and transferred either
to a place of torment or to the Elysian Fields that can be equated
with Paradise. Residents of the Elysian Fields had the possibility

of rebirth once their previous life had been forgotten, a feat achieved by drinking the waters of the River Lethe.

Miraculous powers were associated with the River Styx. Its waters were used by the gods to seal unbreakable oaths, and the Greek hero Achilles was immersed in the river as a child, making him entirely invulnerable except for the spot on his heel where his mother held him for his dip. Achilles eventually lost his life when a poisoned arrow hit him in this heel, an episode that spawned the expression 'Achilles' heel', still used to describe a person's principal weakness.

Traversing a river to the underworld appears in other belief systems. The Sanzu River is the river to cross in the Japanese Buddhist tradition, and the Vaitarna River serves the same purpose in several Hindu religious texts, although only for sinners (those who do good deeds in life do not have to cross the river).

Rivers also feature prominently in accounts of Paradise, in Hebrew, Christian, and Islamic traditions. Early Christians adopted the Hebrew Bible and with it the story of Genesis, in which a single unnamed river is described as flowing out of Eden to water the garden, from where it emerges to feed four rivers. These rivers – the Tigris, Euphrates, Gihon, and Pison – flow to different parts of the world. While the Tigris and Euphrates are known quantities, the Gihon and Pison were a source of wonderment and confusion for many travellers in ancient and medieval times. The Gihon was long associated with Arabia and later became identified as the Ganges or Indus and, on occasion, the Danube. The source of the Gihon, by contrast, was commonly placed in Ethiopia and hence the river was equated with the Nile. The apparent impossibility of such widely disparate rivers as the Tigris, Euphrates, Ganges, and Nile all having a common source in the Garden of Eden was explained by the suggestion that these rivers flowed underground on leaving Eden initially, resurfacing at great distance from Paradise and from each other.

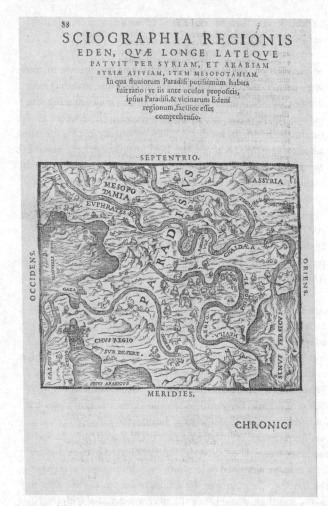

6. Map of the four rivers of Paradise, or Paradisus, published in a 16th-century book, *Chronicum, Scripturae autoritate constitutum*

Four rivers are also specified in the Paradise which the Koran says Allah has prepared for faithful Muslims, a place most frequently described as 'gardens under which rivers flow'. Here the devout are sustained by a river of flowing water, and three others comprising milk, wine, and honey. It is frequently thought that the four rivers of Paradise have exerted a great influence on the design of Islamic gardens, often created as earthly representations of Paradise. Many Islamic gardens are laid out in four sections, divided by channels of water fed from a pool or fountain at the garden's centre, but this four-part design with flowing water playing a defining role actually predates Islam. Hence, it is probably not the layout that reflects a specifically Muslim view of Paradise so much as the description of Paradise that reflects a pre-existing expression of garden form.

Rivers are an important feature in some of the earliest Sanskrit texts from India. One of the most prominent rivers mentioned in the Rig Veda, the first of four books that form the basis for the Hindu religion, is the Sarasvati, a river that is also personified as the goddess Saravati. As a river, the Sarasvati is described as large and fast-flowing in the Rig Veda, but later Hindu texts, including the Mahabharata, depict it as having been reduced to a series of saline lakes. Contemporary interest in the Sarasvati River has led several scholars to equate the mythical river with a number of ancient, dry river channels discovered with the aid of satellite imagery in India's Thar Desert in recent years.

Flood legends

Stories of a great flood crop up with uncanny frequency in the mythology of innumerable cultures, both ancient and modern. The deluge described in the Biblical book of Genesis is well known to many people in the Judaeo-Christian world and has numerous similarities with the flood described in the earlier Babylonian account of the Epic of Gilgamesh and similar stories from Sumeria and Assyria, also in Mesopotamia. The flood is explained as God's way of cleansing the Earth of wayward humanity, although one man and his family manage to escape in a boat, or ark, with representatives of the planet's wildlife population to keep them company. In all of the stories, the ark ends up on a mountain top and birds are sent forth to see whether the floodwaters have receded. The great flood has considerable symbolic significance, involving an obvious cleansing element as well as being a vehicle for rebirth, marking a clear break between the antediluvial and postdiluvial worlds. The event is effectively repeated at the personal level in various ceremonies of purification by water, including the Christian sacrament of baptism, in which the initiate is cleansed of the old ways in the waters of a river (or font) and is reborn in Christ. The ceremony mimics the baptism of Jesus in the River Jordan.

A similar flood-induced divide between a previous world and a new cosmological order appears in the written testimonies of several Maya groups from Central America. In a number of versions, the deluge occurs after a celestial caiman has been decapitated, interpreted as a flood caused by torrential rain. In some accounts, humanity continues thanks to a few survivors, but many other Mesoamerican flood myths, particularly those recorded by the Aztec peoples, tell of no flood survivors so that creation had to start again from the beginning.

A creation myth from Norse mythology tells how the world emerged at the meeting place of fire and ice, a great void into which eleven rivers flowed. An evil frost giant named Ymir sprang from this place and gave birth to the first man and woman from under his left armpit. Eventually, Ymir was killed by gods who created the world out of his body. His skull became the sky; his spilled blood became the Norse flood that drowned all of the frost giants with the exception of one man and his wife, who escaped in a vessel made of a hollowed tree trunk.

Floods also feature in myths and stories told by numerous Aboriginal groups in Australia, their prominence explicable at least in part by the often dramatic nature of flooding in desert landscapes. One story told by the Wiranggu of South Australia tells of a rain-maker named Djunban who was not fully concentrating on his rain-making ceremony one day and brought unusually heavy rain as a result. Djunban tried to warn his people, but a great flood came and washed them away with all their possessions, forming a hill of silt. This is the origin of gold and bones found in the hill.

The possibility that floods described in myths from all over the world are based on real events has on occasion engendered great debates. Deconstruction of the Biblical flood story, for example, played a central role in the rise of scientific geology in the 19th century. The British geologist Charles Lyell, in his influential book *The Principles of Geology* (published in three volumes, 1830–3), dismissed the prevailing belief in Noah's flood due to a lack of evidence in the geological record. Lyell's book was one of the key works in a struggle between science and faith as the predominant basis for explaining the origins of the world around us. It led to a widespread understanding that our planet is very much older than creationists believed.

Sacred rivers

Many belief systems have invested elements of the natural world with sacred characteristics, and specific rivers feature prominently among them. Rivers were sacred to the Celts of northwestern Europe, for instance, and many were personified as goddesses. Some of the river names used today in this part of the world can be traced back to the Celtic deities who lived near them or died in them. In Ireland, the Rivers Boyne and Shannon derive their names from goddesses who drowned in them after seeking wisdom from a magical well.

The importance of the Nile to the ancient Egyptians was reflected in a number of major and minor gods being associated with the river. Hapi was the god who personified the river's annual flood, the inundation of tears shed each year by the goddess Isis, in sorrow for her murdered husband. Hapi, the Nile deity responsible for collecting these tears, lived in a cataract near today's Aswan, surrounded by crocodiles and goddesses, some of whom were frogs, others women with frogs' heads. Each year, at the start of the flood, Egyptians carried out mass animal sacrifices to Hapi.

In numerous cases, the sanctity of a river is linked to a creation myth that arises from water's position as a primordial element. The River Birem in Ghana, for example, is considered to be the spiritual force and fountainhead of the Akyem kingdom because legend has it that the people of Akyem emerged from the depths of the river. Indeed, rivers, streams, and other water bodies all across Africa are frequently regarded as the habitat of deities and ancestors and hence treated with considerable reverence. The most prominent of the river divinities in Yoruba cosmology, for instance, is Yemoja, ruler of the Ogun River in Nigeria. Yemoja is the mother of all fish and the giver of children, and is customarily brought offerings of yams and chickens by women who want to start a family. In many parts of southern Africa, spirits who dwell in certain river pools are responsible for the creation of traditional healers (see below).

Many of the indigenous peoples of Siberia also traditionally enjoy close links to nature, in which rivers and other elements of the landscape are central to their animistic spiritual belief systems. Rivers, springs, lakes, and mountains are understood to have spirit-guardians whose presence must be regularly acknowledged and honoured via a community's shaman. For example, the Katun River is considered central to the culture of the indigenous Altaians who inhabit the Russian Altai region on the confluence of its borders with Kazakhstan, China, and Mongolia. Altaians consider the Katun to be a living being, and show appropriate respect in several ways. These include not throwing stones into the river, saying special words when crossing it, and not taking water from the Katun at night because this may upset the river's spirit.

A similar attitude toward rivers is found among the Mansi who live in the Tyumen region of northwestern Siberia. Sacred rivers such as the Yalbynya must not be fished, and even rowing a boat is prohibited in some stretches, so the vessel has to be pulled along from the bank. Other reaches come with different embargoes: the extraction of drinking water is forbidden, for example, or felling trees on certain banks. The river mouth is considered to be the most significant part of the Yalbynya, where local people throw money on passing.

In southeastern Europe, the waters of the Danube play an important part in traditional funeral customs practised by Bulgarians and Romanians living along the river's lower reaches. The river has considerable symbolic value for the idea of death as a long journey to the nether world and is incorporated into often elaborate memorial rituals. 'Freeing the water' of the deceased is a rite that provides water to the dead person for use in the afterlife. The ritual, which varies in detail from village to village, usually involves a child bringing river water to certain houses. In the Bulgarian village of Leskovec, the child is a girl who then returns to the Danube with several women where they lay down a tablecloth on the riverbank and set out a meal consisting of boiled wheat and wine. The women light a candle and hang gifts for the child on a forked stick taken from an apple tree. The girl puts her right foot in the river and asks three times for the ceremony to be witnessed, at which point a hollowed pumpkin containing a candle, some wheat, and a piece of bread is launched from the riverbank. When the pumpkin floats away down the Danube, the water will reach the deceased, but should the pumpkin turn over, the deceased will be angry.

Rivers feature among the most important types of sacred place in Hinduism. About 3,000 years ago, rivers were revered by the

Aryan people of the Vedic period in the region that is now India, and evidence from archaeological excavations suggests that the Hindu practice of mass bathing in rivers on auspicious occasions dates back to (and derives from) a similar practice in the Harappan civilization of the Indus Valley, up to 2,000 years before that. Indeed, the words 'Hindu' and 'India' are derived from the Indus.

Virtually all Indian rivers are revered as deities, but the Indus is commonly referred to as one of the seven holy rivers of India, the others being the Ganges, Yamuna (or Jumna), Sarasvati, Godavari, Narmada, and Kaveri. However, the Indus and the Kaveri are occasionally replaced by the Tapti and the Kistna. The rivers are often thought of as the veins in the earth's body, and many specific places along a river's course are particularly sacred, including the source, mouth, and confluences. The most sacred of all India's holy rivers is the Ganges.

The Ganges

The connections Hindus have with the Ganges provide one of the most striking examples of the sanctity of rivers. Indeed, in India 'Ganga' is both the name of the River Ganges and the personification of the river as a goddess. The holiness of the Ganges is enshrined in numerous Hindu epics and scriptures, including the Ramayana, the Mahabharata, the Vedas, and the Puranas. The story of the river's arrival on Earth from the heavens has it that the feat was achieved by a sage, known as Bhagiratha, who went to the Himalayan mountains and managed to persuade the river to descend. In several versions of the story, it is the god Shiva who controls the flow of the river, and Gangadhara, or 'Bearer of the Ganges', is one of Shiva's other names.

The water of the Ganges has numerous auspicious properties for Hindus. It acts as a medicine for every ailment, and bathing in it cleanses the devoted from all sin. Crucially, however, when a person's ashes or bones are entrusted to the river, the soul will be released for rebirth. For many Hindus, the holy city of Varanasi is the preferred place for this final transformation. The west bank of the Ganges at Varanasi is divided into many sections of river frontage each consisting of a series of long steps down to the water, the 'ghats' where people come to bathe, wash their clothes, and cremate the dead. About 80 corpses a day are burned at the two main ghats in Varanasi, most of these brought to the river from outside the city. The ashes of many more people are brought for final immersion in the Ganges. Some corpses that are not cremated, such as those who had smallpox in the past or who died of cholera, are simply weighted down and submerged in the holy waters. Among the most important ghats that specialize in cremation is Manikarnika, which contains the well dug at the beginning of time by Vishnu, one of the most significant Hindu deities who is sometimes depicted as a man-fish. This is the place where all creation, or the cosmos, will burn at the end of time.

Another of the Ganges' most sacred places occurs at its confluence with the Yamuna River, a pilgrimage site popularly known as Prayag, near today's city of Allahabad. This is one of four sites of the mass Hindu pilgrimage Kumbh Mela. According to legend, this is also the place where the mythical Saraswati River joins the Ganges and Yamuna Rivers, thus lending the confluence an additional level of sanctity. The full Kumbh Mela, in which many millions of devotees bathe in the Ganges to purify their sins, takes place every 12 years. The event in 2001 was thought to have been attended by some 60 million people, making it the world's largest gathering in recorded history.

Sacred river creatures

Given the reverence with which numerous rivers are viewed by peoples all over the world, it should come as no surprise to learn that some of the creatures found in rivers have also been the objects of respect and veneration. Certain types of fish found in

7. Kumbh Mela, the mass Hindu pilgrimage to the sacred Ganges

the Nile were surrounded by mythology and superstition in ancient Egypt, where some species were sacred in particular settlements but not in others. The mormyrus, recognizable by its lengthy down-turned snout, was revered in the city of Oxyrhynchus, where it was never eaten, and considerable numbers of mormyrus have been found mummified in tombs in the Oxyrhynchus area. The Greek historian Plutarch tells how the fish sparked a violent confrontation between the inhabitants of Oxyrhynchus and the nearby city of Cynopolis after the people of Cynopolis, where the dog was held sacred, were one day seen eating mormyrus. The citizens of Oxyrhynchus rounded up all the dogs they could find and ate them in retaliation.

River dolphins have been venerated in several parts of the world. The South Asian river dolphin of the sacred Ganges was given religious significance with its mention in the Rig Veda and became one of the first protected species in history. It was accorded a special status under the reign of Emperor Ashoka, one of India's most famous rulers, in the 3rd century BC. In South-East Asia, both the Khmer and Lao people regard the Irrawaddy dolphin as a sacred animal, and they are rarely hunted. Likewise, in South American Indian folklore, the Amazon river dolphin is considered sacred, leading to the belief that hunting and killing them will bring bad luck. The Yangtze river dolphin was revered as the goddess of the Yangtze in China until it was declared extinct in 2007.

Various species of salmon have been honoured in myths and rituals in several societies thanks to their value as an important seasonal food source and their ability to survive in both the salty ocean and freshwater rivers. The Atlantic salmon occupied a special place in Celtic mythology. It was said to be as old as time and to know all things, both in the past and in the future. The Salmon of Wisdom, from Irish legend, features in an important episode in the early life of Fionn mac Cumhaill (anglicized to Finn McCool), a legendary hunter-warrior. Fionn was studying under a poet who had sought the fish for seven years. When the poet finally caught the fish, he asked Fionn to cook it for him, but Fionn burned his thumb on the fish and instinctively put it in his mouth to suck the burn, hence receiving all the knowledge in the world.

During the Middle Ages in Britain, salmon were known as the all-knowing water creatures in Arthurian legends. Gwrhyr, one of King Arthur's finest men and an expert linguist, talked to a series of wise animals in his search for a master huntsman. Each animal was wiser than the previous one, and the oldest and wisest of them all was the salmon of Llyn Llyw, a mythological pool on the River Severn. The magic salmon was said to have gained the power of wisdom by consuming hazelnuts that had dropped into its pool. According to this tradition, the number of spots on a salmon's back is supposed to represent the number of nuts consumed.

Salmon has long been a principal source of food for indigenous groups in northern latitudes, such as on the Pacific coast of North America before the arrival of European colonists. As such a mainstay of the diet, the fish became a focus for numerous rituals, taboos, and mythological stories. Catching the salmon as they ran up the rivers in enormous numbers to spawn was a time of great abundance, often marking a stark contrast to the times when only dried meat and fish were eaten, so the start of the season was a time for reverence and celebration. In the early decades of the 20th century, anthropologists working in the region recorded details of the 'first salmon ceremony' held among many Native American groups, to mark the initial salmon run of the season, before the practice ceased.

Among the Tsimshian communities along the Skeena River in today's Canadian province of British Columbia, any fisherman landing the first salmon was obliged to call four shamans who arrived to take charge. The fish was placed on a mat made of cedar bark and carried to the chief's house in a procession led by one of the shaman – who had put on the fisherman's clothing – holding a rattle in his right hand and an eagle's tail in the left. At the house, in the presence of senior members of the community, the shamans would march around the salmon four times before the man wearing the fisherman's clothes called for the fish's head to be severed, followed by its tail, and the removal of its stomach. The ceremony, marked by the chanting of honorary names, was conducted with a mussel-shell knife. It was thought that using a stone or metal knife would cause a thunderstorm.

Similar first salmon ceremonies were conducted up and down the Pacific seaboard with only minor differences. Some involved speeches and feasting, others ceremonial dances. All stressed respect for the salmon in the hope that it would come in great numbers. Salmon was eaten fresh during the fishing season and dried or smoked for the winter food supply. Many groups in North America, Siberia, and northeastern China also used salmon skin to make their clothing.

River spirits

The association between rivers and various mythical creatures is common to numerous cultures all over the world. In Germanic and Nordic folklore, such water sprites are known as 'nixie' (singular nix) and usually have evil intentions. They frequently entice their human victims to join them, luring them into the water, from which there is no escape. The nix may take different forms, either male or female. One of the best known from Germany was Lorelei, a beautiful nymph who sat on a rock in the Rhine which now bears her name, and lured fishermen into danger with the sound of her voice or by combing her hair. Scandinavian nixie were more likely to be male, drawing their female victims into a river or lake with enchanting songs played on the violin. Pregnant women and unbaptized children were especially vulnerable.

Another form of river spirit in Scandinavian folklore is the bäckahästen, or 'brook horse', a majestic white beast that would commonly appear on river banks, especially during foggy weather, presenting a tempting ride for a weary traveller. Anyone who climbed onto its back would be unable to dismount, enabling the horse to jump into the river and drown its rider. The kelpie of Scottish folklore is a direct parallel of the bäckahästen. Its most common guise was that of a fine-looking tame horse, but the kelpie could also appear as a hairy man with a terrible vice-like grip. He would hide on the river bank until an unfortunate traveller was passing and then leap out to crush the life from him.

A spirit associated with rivers all over Japan is the kappa, a mischievous creature often described as something between a child and a monkey. One of the kappa's favourite tricks is also to lure people, horses, or cattle into a river to drown. There are numerous regional variations to the kappa and its behaviour, but one of its most common traits is an affinity for cucumbers (frequently thought of as a symbol of fertility). In some parts of Japan, it is believed that anyone eating a cucumber before swimming will certainly be attacked by a kappa, although in other areas it is a way to ensure protection against kappa attack. Either way, many festivals associated with kappa include offerings of cucumbers, and the link between the kappa and the cucumber continues in modern Japan through the name of a type of sushi made with cucumbers: kappa maki. Interestingly, the character of the centuries-old kappa has been subject to a make-over in the last hundred years or so, and has been transformed from a malicious and unpleasant water deity into a harmless and endearing mascot. As a nationally recognized symbol, the kappa has been used for various campaigns that draw on a nostalgia for Japan's rural past. It is ironic to note that one of these was a clean water campaign aiming to regenerate the environment around urban rivers, calling for rivers to be cleaned up so that kappa will come back.

Traditionally, the kappa, like the nix, bäckahästen, and kelpie, are malevolent river spirits, luring the unwary to a watery death. In southern Africa, by contrast, the spirits associated with river systems and other water bodies in the traditional cosmologies of Khoisan- and Bantu-speaking indigenous peoples behave rather differently. To many of these groups, water spirits are regarded as ancestors and they prefer to live in certain spots. In rivers, these are deep pools, frequently below waterfalls where the water is fast-moving and 'living', often generating lots of foam. These spirits take on various zoomorphic manifestations, primarily the snake and the mermaid. They interact with humans in a variety of ways, and one of the most important of these is their fundamental importance to traditional healing and its practitioners.

Water spirits traditionally call certain chosen individuals to become diviners or healers, which usually involves the physical submersion of the candidate under the water of a certain river pool for a few hours, days, or even years. When the man or woman emerges from the depths, he or she is wearing a snake and has acquired psychic abilities and healing skills, including knowledge of medicinal plants. This experience of being taken under the water can occur in a dream, but this is simply notification that the ancestors are calling the individual to become a healer. The calling frequently comes after a period of illness, although when children are called, they often just happen to be playing near the river at the time. Resistance to this calling is not advised and usually leads to misfortune. Relatives are not allowed to display any grief at the disappearance of one who has gone under the water or the individual may never be returned.

Given the importance of the water spirits, many rivers, pools, and water sources are viewed with a mixture of awe, fear, and respect by indigenous communities in southern Africa. Their sanctity has generated numerous taboos surrounding access and use. Frequently, only healers, kings, and chiefs are allowed to approach such areas. The general populace is forbidden to go near sacred pools for fear of being taken under the water, never to return. Such taboos represent just one small fragment of the great web of influence rivers exert on humankind, a power that can be traced back to the beginnings of humanity. The ways in which the flow of rivers has helped to shape history is investigated in more detail in the following chapter.

Chapter 3
Liquid histories

> I have seen the Mississippi. That is muddy water. I have seen the St
> Lawrence. That is crystal water. But the Thames is liquid history.
>
> John Burns (1858–1943)
> (British politician)

Rivers reflect history. They also help to create it. Societies interact with
rivers for many reasons, and these motivations can be classified simply
into those rooted in the useful aspects of rivers and those that reflect
rivers as hazards. People derive many benefits from rivers. We have
caught and eaten fish from them for tens of thousands of years. Rivers
provide water for domestic, industrial, and agricultural uses. They also
provide all sorts of minerals, ranging from gold and diamonds to the
sand and gravel that is so essential to modern construction. The
energy in a flowing river can be harnessed to facilitate trade and
travel, to generate electricity, and to remove many types of waste
produced by human activities. People enjoy rivers for recreational and
aesthetic reasons, and as havens for wildlife. Conversely, rivers can
breed fear and trepidation. This may be a function of quantity: either
too much water – a flood; or too little – a water shortage. The quality
of river water may also be a cause for concern, as a bearer of disease or
dangerous concentrations of minerals such as arsenic.

All of these facets of rivers as perceived by society have inevitably
had some bearing on the course of human history. Much of Europe's

story can be told through the story of the Danube. The rivers of Bangladesh compose both the landscape of the nation and the life of its people. London is nothing without the Thames. Rivers are an essential part of the very fabric of many societies and their histories.

The first civilizations

Ancient civilizations emerged on the floodplains of large rivers in several parts of the world between 3,500 and 5,500 years ago. The appearance of the Sumerian, Egyptian, and Harappan civilizations along the alluvial valleys of the Tigris-Euphrates, the Nile, and the Indus respectively was due in large part to the key benefits offered by their rivers: an abundant supply of fresh water, fertile alluvial soils, and a ready transport corridor for trade and travellers. In each case, the society's reliance on its river was emphasized by the arid location, making inhabitants particularly dependent upon a reliable flow of water for agriculture and their continued existence in a desert environment. All three river systems are exotic: rising in areas with more humid climates which maintain their perennial flow through the desert.

One theory linking many of the factors involved in the emergence of these first civilizations suggests that the central organization required to manage irrigation in desert areas also allowed complex societies to evolve as large numbers of people congregated to live in the same place. This tendency led eventually to the creation of the first cities and what are popularly thought of as the first civilizations. Each of these three early river-based civilizations developed its own ways of diverting and channelling water, growing and storing food. Systems for writing, making laws, and many other hallmarks of civilization also emerged separately in these three regions. This theory of 'hydraulic civilizations' suggests that the deliberate manipulation and regulation of their rivers by these early societies was an inherent and necessary precondition of civilization.

Another idea takes the links between these early complex societies and their rivers a step further, to suggest that the nature, character, and longevity of the civilization was in part a reflection of the nature of its river. The Tigris-Euphrates, Nile, and Indus are all large, exotic river systems, but in other respects they are quite different. The Nile has a relatively gentle gradient in Egypt and a channel that has experienced only small changes over the last few thousand years, by meander cut-off and a minor shift eastwards. The river usually flooded in a regular and predictable way. The stability and long continuity of the Egyptian civilization may be a reflection of its river's relative stability. The steeper channel of the Indus, by contrast, has experienced major avulsions over great distances on the lower Indus Plain and some very large floods caused by the failure of glacier ice dams in the Himalayan mountains. Likely explanations for the abandonment of many Harappan cities, including Mohenjo Daro, take account of damage caused by major floods and/or the disruption caused by channel avulsion leading to a loss of water supply.

Channel avulsion was also a problem for the Sumerian civilization on the alluvial plain called Mesopotamia – 'the land between two rivers' – known for the rise and fall of its numerous city states. Most of these cities were situated along the Euphrates River, probably because it was more easily controlled for irrigation purposes than the Tigris, which flowed faster and carried much more water. However, the Euphrates was an anastomosing river with multiple channels that diverge and rejoin. Over time, individual branch channels ceased to flow as others formed, and settlements located on these channels inevitably declined and were abandoned as their water supply ran dry, while others expanded as their channels carried greater amounts of water.

Pathways for exploration

The straightforward pathways offered by rivers have always been used by people arriving to explore new lands. Archaeological evidence suggests that early humans penetrated an island later to become known as Britain along its major rivers during the

Palaeolithic period or early Stone Age, later spreading out and settling areas further from the river banks. Similarly, some 6,000 years ago, Neolithic tribes used river courses to enter Central Europe from the southeast. In both cases, river valleys offered plentiful supplies of essential resources for these early settlers: water, fish, and floodplains rich in game for hunting.

Many hundreds of years later, the great river systems of North America enabled European pioneers to explore vast new territories, opening them up to trade and eventual colonization. In the 16th century, a succession of French traders, explorers, and missionaries were the first Europeans to arrive in the Great Lakes region, following the exploration of the St Lawrence River by their fellow countryman Jacques Cartier in the 1530s. Dispatched by the king of France, their main purpose was to chart the river systems as highways that allowed access to a new continent. These were often the only thoroughfares through the otherwise impenetrable forests of North America, traversable by canoe as liquid highways or dogsled when many tributaries froze over during the winter.

By 1804, when Meriwether Lewis and William Clark were sent by US president Thomas Jefferson to explore, survey, and document an immense swathe of North America that he'd just bought from the French – the Louisiana Purchase – rivers were still the easiest routes to follow. Lewis and Clark's expedition took them up the Missouri River, across the Rocky Mountains, and down the Columbia River to the Pacific Ocean. Their expedition and the information they brought back, particularly about the Pacific northwest, played a pivotal part in the westward thrust of US expansion.

Movement along rivers played a similar role in the expansion of Russian power and influence over Siberia and the penetration of Africa by Western European powers. The importance of rivers as pathways for colonial exploration is not simply a subject of historical interest. During the colonization of the Americas in the mid-18th century and the imperial expansion into Africa and Asia in the late 19th century, rivers were commonly used as boundaries because they were the first, and frequently the only, features mapped by European explorers. The diplomats in Europe who negotiated the allocation of colonial territories claimed by rival powers knew little of the places they were carving up. Often, their limited knowledge was based solely on maps that showed few details, rivers being the only distinct physical features marked. Today, many international river boundaries remain as legacies of those historical decisions based on poor geographical knowledge because states have been reluctant to alter their territorial boundaries from original delimitation agreements.

Australia's Murray River

The Murray River in the southeast of Australia is of immense cultural, economic, and environmental importance to the continent. Its significance becomes greater still if its two largest tributaries, the Murrumbidgee and Darling Rivers, are included. Altogether, the Murray-Darling Basin drains about 14% of Australia's total land area. Numerous Aboriginal peoples relied on the abundance of the river for thousands of years before the arrival of Europeans, hunting and trading along the Murray in canoes cut and shaped from the bark of gum trees growing on the river's edge. Rock art, archaeological and burial sites remain as evidence of these early inhabitants. Their diet from the river was varied, including fish, crayfish, mussels, frogs, turtles, and waterfowl and their eggs.

It was not until the 1820s that European explorers first saw the river. Captain Charles Sturt navigated down the Murrumbidgee, followed the Murray to discover the Darling confluence, and continued downriver to the mouth of the great river. Publication in London of Sturt's account of his river exploration led indirectly to the establishment of the colony of South Australia. Early

European settlers began to penetrate the continent's interior by following the Murray and small settlements and sheep farms started to spring up along its banks. One of the most memorable symbols of the European history of the Murray River is the paddle-steamer, numbers of which ferried wool, wheat, and other goods up and down the river system, helping to open up the Murray-Darling Basin. Irrigated agriculture began in 1887, accelerating settlement and exploitation of the river's water supplies.

Today, the Murray-Darling Basin is Australia's most important agricultural area, producing over one-third of the nation's food supply. It contains 65% of the country's irrigated farmland and supports more than one-quarter of the national cattle herd and nearly half of its sheep. It also provides water to major cities including Canberra and Adelaide. In its natural state, however, the River Murray was a highly variable and unpredictable source of water. During severe droughts, it ceased to be a river at all and was transformed into a chain of salty waterholes, but flow has been regulated for many years to maintain a reliable supply. River regulation on the Murray has been achieved with an array of water engineering structures and techniques. They include five main water storage points, including two large dams – Dartmouth and Hume – and the major managed lakes of Mulwala, Victoria, and Menindee. Since the Hume Dam was completed in 1936, a continuous flow has been maintained throughout the length of the river. The Murray and the Murrumbidgee Rivers also receive additional water supplies diverted through a series of tunnels and pipes from the Snowy River. A system of thirteen weirs and locks further aids flow regulation, and five barrages have been constructed near the river mouth to prevent the intrusion of sea water. Salt occurs naturally in the Murray-Darling Basin in large quantities, and is a water-quality issue for domestic and agricultural use. Hence, a series of salt-interception schemes has been established to keep salt out of the river. These schemes involve large-scale groundwater pumping and drainage projects that intercept flows of saline water and dispose of them by evaporation.

Natural barriers

There are many examples of rivers acting as natural barriers to interaction between groups, and in some cases the separation has continued over periods long enough to be apparent in genetic studies. Among primates in Central Africa, the Congo River forms a clear divide between bonobos, or pygmy chimpanzees, which are found only on the south side of the Congo, and common chimpanzees, which occur only to the north. Chimpanzees are not known to swim, so the river has effectively isolated the two groups, for about 1.3 million years according to genetic analysis, which also confirms that they have a common ancestry.

Similar river barriers to the flow of genes, cultures, and languages have been identified in some human societies. A classic case has been documented by anthropologists in the Highlands of New Guinea where the Lamari River marks a very sharp cultural and linguistic divide between the Fore and the Anga. These two groups speak completely unrelated languages and have markedly different cultures. They are also mortal enemies. Although there may be several reasons for their differences, the formidable natural barrier presented by the Lamari River and its precipitous valley is certainly an important one, particularly given that the Fore believe people to be incapable of swimming.

Rivers have always demarcated such boundaries, both real and imagined. The River Danube in Europe marked the northern frontier of the Roman Empire in the 1st century AD because it was easily defended, hence also drawing a perceived line between the 'civilized' Empire and the barbarian tribes on the bank opposite. In Europe today, the Danube marks the international border between Slovakia and Hungary, and stretches of Romania's borders with Serbia, Bulgaria, and Ukraine. In southern Germany, the Danube is affectionately known to most Bavarians as the 'Weisswurst equator' (literally, the 'white sausage equator', named after a favourite food from the south), the symbolic borderline between themselves and the different cultures to the north.

The importance of rivers as natural barriers is reflected in the fact that no less than three-quarters of the world's international boundaries follow rivers for at least part of their course. However, rivers are also notoriously erratic boundaries thanks to their inherent tendency to move, a propensity that can result in a multitude of legal, technical, and managerial challenges for rival states on opposing banks.

These are challenges both in terms of identifying a definitive line in a dynamic natural feature and of managing a divided transboundary water resource. The two elements are of course related: deciding where exactly the boundary runs affects legal rights to the water itself and how it is used (e.g. for navigation) or abused (e.g. by pollution). Often, a river boundary follows the 'thalweg', the deepest channel in the river, but other principles are also used. Some boundaries follow the median line between the banks, or lines drawn between turning points. Others follow one of the river banks. On occasion, two countries may favour two different legal principles for determining the position of the border, often for opportunistic reasons, and the resulting dispute frequently has to be resolved by international adjudication. Even after the border has been agreed, erosion and sedimentation can alter the banks, the median, or the thalweg, to the benefit of one country and the detriment of the other.

The International Boundary and Water Commission between Mexico and the USA is a long-standing example of the interrelationship between river boundary identification and river management. The commission was created in 1884 to demarcate the border on the ground and to identify its position in the Tijuana, Colorado, and Rio Grande Rivers, but in 1944 it was also given responsibility for allocating the water resources of the Rio Grande. Today, the International Boundary and Water Commission spends most of its time on water management and allocation, rather than on boundary definition. Not all river boundary disputes are settled by peaceful negotiation, however. In 1969, about 3,000 troops from the Soviet Union and China lost their lives in a fierce conflict lasting several months over their international boundary along the Ussuri River and specifically over the ownership of Chenpao island.

River rights and conflicts

The importance of fresh water as a resource, allied to its uneven geographical distribution in rivers, lakes, and underground aquifers, has inevitably led to political wrangling over the rights of different groups to use water. On occasion, disagreement over rights to shared water resources can lead to militarized confrontation, and the notion that so-called 'water wars' may become a leading source of conflict in the 21st century has become quite widespread in some academic and journalistic circles, as well as in political rhetoric.

Many rivers flow across (as well as along) the borders between nation states, and approximately 60% of the world's fresh water is drawn from rivers shared by more than one country. Some of the world's larger river basins are shared by a great number of countries. The Danube is the greatest of them all in this regard, its basin being shared by no fewer than nineteen countries in Europe. Five other basins – the Congo, Niger, Nile, Rhine, and Zambezi – are shared by between nine and eleven countries. These facts suggest the scale of possible river rights issues, although multiple stake-holders are by no means necessary for political discontent. The River Ganges, for example, flows through just two countries yet was the subject of a twenty-year confrontation between India and Bangladesh following completion of India's Farakka Barrage in 1975. Bangladesh complained that it was being deprived of water it could use for irrigation and was subject to increasing salinity problems thanks to diversions of water by the barrage, sited some 18 kilometres upstream from its border with India.

The dispute over the Ganges, which eventually resulted in the signing of a water-sharing accord in 1996, is not atypical. A downstream state's objection to pollution, the construction of a dam, or excessive irrigation by an upstream state, actions which will decrease or degrade the quality of water available to the downstream state, are all classic grounds for disagreement over a cross-border river. Many of these disputes are peacefully settled by international treaty, but many are not. Further, not all international treaties are designed to address all players in an international river dispute. An example here can be quoted from the Nile. Egypt and Sudan have an international agreement that governs the volume of Nile water allowed to pass through the Aswan High Dam, but none of the other eight Nile Basin countries have agreements over use of the Nile's waters. Given that Egypt and Sudan are the last two states through which the river flows before entering the Mediterranean, similar agreement over water rights with countries further upstream would seem desirable. Hammering out the details of such a treaty has, to date, proved insurmountable, and differences in opinion over rights to Nile water continue to underlie many of the political issues in this part of the world.

Agreements to resolve disputes over water resources have a very long history. The beginnings of international water law can be traced back at least to 2500 BC, when two Sumerian city states – Lagash and Umma – reached an agreement to end a dispute over the water resources of a tributary of the River Tigris in the Middle East. Wrangles over water are still a significant potential source of conflict in the Tigris-Euphrates Basin due to a lack of agreements in the contemporary era. While there is currently a water surplus in this region, the scale of planned developments has raised concerns. The Southeastern Anatolian Project in Turkey, a regional development scheme on the headwaters of the two rivers, envisages the eventual construction of 22 dams. In 1990, when the reservoir behind the Ataturk Dam began to fill, stemming the flow of the Euphrates, immediate alarm was expressed by Syria and Iraq, despite the fact that governments in both countries had been alerted and discharge before the cut-off had been enhanced in compensation. Full development of the Southeastern Anatolian Project, expected by about 2030, could reduce the flow of the Euphrates by as much as 60%, which could severely jeopardize Syrian and Iraqi agriculture downstream. The three Tigris–Euphrates riparians have tried to reach agreements over the water use from these two rivers, and the need for such an agreement is becoming more pressing.

Force has been used in conflicts over scarce water resources elsewhere in the Middle East. Attempts to divert water from the Jordan and Yarmuk Rivers led to multiple military incidents between Israel, Syria, and Jordan in the 1950s and 1960s. In 1967, just before the Six-Day War between Israel and its Arab neighbours, then prime minister Levi Eshkol declared that 'water is a question of survival for Israel', and that Israel would use 'all means necessary to secure that the water continues to flow'.

Since then, the spectre of 'water wars' has assumed greater prominence in popular views of how relations between states sharing a river basin, particularly those in the Middle East, will develop in the future. However, not all authorities see more inter-state conflicts as either inevitable or even the most important aspect of transboundary river management. National economic development is just one dimension of 'water security', the idea of sustainable access to adequate quantities of water, of acceptable quality, for multiple uses. Such uses also include social and cultural needs but important ecosystem functions too. All of these users should have rights to a river and hence conflicts between them can emerge at levels other than the nation state.

The Mekong Basin illustrates this point. Like many of the world's international river basins, it is simultaneously viewed as an engine of regional economic development, as a crucial basis of livelihood resources, and also as a vital site for the conservation of biodiversity. Critics of the 1995 Mekong Agreement between four of the basin's nation states see the treaty as overly focused on the Mekong's huge hydroelectric potential and capacity to store water for irrigation schemes. Development of this potential is inevitably concentrated at the national level, often with assistance from international development partners such as banks and other governments. These bodies, it is argued, view the Mekong's resources as under-utilized and ripe for development, but the fear is that this stance will marginalize the activities of local resource-users who depend on the river for sustenance and livelihoods.

Muddy history

The sediments carried in rivers, laid down over many years, represent a record of the changes that have occurred in the drainage basin through the ages. Analysis of these sediments is one way in which physical geographers can interpret the historical development of landscapes. They can study the physical and chemical characteristics of the sediment itself and/or the biological remains they contain, such as pollen or spores. In some places, the sediments may be exposed in a free-face – naturally, such as a cliff, or thanks to human action – and can be examined and sampled fairly easily, but in most cases the sequence of sediments is sampled from the top down, back through time, using a device that drills a core.

The simple rate at which material is deposited by a river can be a good reflection of how conditions have changed in the drainage basin. For example, a study of sediment laid down over a period of 300 years by the Bush River, which flows into Chesapeake Bay on the eastern seaboard of North America, has shown that the amount of soil eroded from the catchment has altered significantly in response to changing land use in the area. Before the settlement of Europeans in the Bush River basin, which began in the mid-17th century, native populations are thought to have had no significant environmental impact on the basin, and the sedimentation rate before 1750 was about 1 millimetre per year. However, the rate was eight times greater by 1820 thanks to early deforestation and agriculture practised by the first Europeans. As the felling of trees progressed and agriculture intensified over the next 100 years, greater erosion followed, and sedimentation rates peaked in 1850 at about 35 millimetres per year. In more recent times, since 1920, urbanization – protecting soils – and the building of dams – blocking the delivery of sediment – have combined to reduce erosion and sedimentation by an order of magnitude. The sedimentation rate has been reduced nearly to the background conditions that prevailed in the pre-European settlement era.

Pollen from surrounding plants is often found in abundance in fluvial sediments, and the analysis of pollen can yield a great deal of information about past conditions in an area. The type of vegetation can be modified by all sorts of factors, including human interference as in the Bush River basin example, but also for entirely natural reasons such as a change in climate or soil conditions. Very long sediment cores taken from lakes and swamps enable us to reconstruct changes in vegetation over very long time periods, in some cases over a million years and more. Because climate is a strong determinant of vegetation, pollen analysis has also proved to be an important method for tracing changes in past climates.

An important study of a 250-metre-long core from the bed of Lake Biwa in Japan, for instance, showed changes in pollen over about the last 430,000 years, a period in which five glacial–interglacial cycles could be recognized. During glacial periods, pollen from pine, birch, and quercus (or white oak) trees was dominant, indicating a climate that was cool and temperate, tending towards subarctic. During interglacial periods, by contrast, high pollen values for species typical of a warm–temperate climate were found, including broad-leaved trees such as the deciduous Lagerstroemia (or Crape myrtle) and the evergreen Castanopsis (a type of beech).

Other evidence for environmental change can be detected in larger-scale elements of the landscape. The floodplains of many modern rivers, for example, bear traces of former channels, so-called 'palaeochannels', which are different in scale and/or form from the current river. If a palaeochannel is buried beneath more recent sediments, it was probably formed by a river that flowed towards a lower base level, indicating that local sea level or lake level has subsequently changed. River terraces that are found in many river valleys are thought to reflect fluctuations of climate, their formation having been driven by the direct and indirect influence of temperature and precipitation on fluvial activity.

Water power

The energy in flowing and falling water has been harnessed to perform work by turning waterwheels for more than 2,000 years. The moving water turns a large wheel and a shaft connected to the wheel axle transmits the power from the water through a system of gears and cogs to work machinery, such as a millstone to grind corn. An early description of a water-powered mill for grinding grain is given by a Roman engineer named Vitruvius, who compiled a treatise in ten volumes covering all aspects of Roman engineering, and the eastern Mediterranean is strongly associated with the first use of this technology, although a separate tradition of using water power also emerged at about the same time in China. Roman waterwheels were frequently connected to other forms of hydraulic engineering, such as aqueducts and dams, designed to transport river water and control its flow to the wheels. Multiple sets of Roman watermills for grinding grain into flour on a large scale are known from the Krokodilion River near

Caesarea Maritima in today's Israel, and from Chemtou and Testour on the River Medjerda (the ancient Bagradas River) in the Roman cornbelt of North Africa, part of Tunisia today. The mills just outside the town of Caesarea Maritima consisted of four vertical waterwheels fed by an aqueduct from a dam on the river.

The power of rivers became widely used in the ancient world for milling grain but also for other purposes. Water-powered mills were also developed to drive trip-hammers for crushing ore and saws for cutting rock. All sorts of water-powered machines became more and more common in medieval Europe, gradually taking over tasks from manual labour. The early medieval watermill was able to do the work of between 30 and 60 people, and by the end of the 10th century in Europe, waterwheels were commonly used in a wide range of industries, including powering forge hammers, oil and silk mills, sugar-cane crushers, ore-crushing mills, breaking up bark in tanning mills, pounding leather, and grinding stones. Nonetheless, most were still used for grinding grains for preparation into various types of food and drink. The Domesday Book, a survey prepared in England in AD 1086, lists 6,082 watermills, although this is probably a conservative estimate because many mills were not recorded in the far north of the country. By 1300, this number had risen to exceed 10,000.

All across Europe, the watermills generally belonged to lords, to city corporations, or to churches or monasteries. Cistercian monasteries were instrumental in the initial development in England of the 'fulling' mill in the late 12th century. Fulling, or felting, was one in a sequence of processes during the production of woollen cloth produced on the monastic estates. It involved scouring and consolidation of the fibres of the fabric, both necessary for proper finishing. The introduction of water-powered technology revolutionized fulling, a process that had hitherto relied on human power to beat the cloth. On the Isle of Wight in southern England, for instance, the first fulling mill was established at the Cistercian monastery of Quarr Abbey on a stream close to large areas of pasture on the abbey's estates. Wool from the flocks of sheep was processed at the abbey and sold in nearby towns.

Medieval watermills typically powered their wheels by using a dam or weir to concentrate the falling water and pond a reserve supply. These modifications to rivers became increasingly common all over Europe, and by the end of the Middle Ages, in the mid-15th century, watermills were in use on a huge number of rivers and streams. The importance of water power continued into the Industrial Revolution, when a series of inventions transformed the manufacture of cotton in England and gave rise to a new mode of production: the factory system. The early textile factories were built to produce cloth using machines driven by waterwheels, so they were often called mills.

The supremacy of running water was soon superseded by steam power generated by burning charcoal, coal, and later oil and gas, although rivers have continued to play a role in industrial power generation. All thermal electric generating stations, whether the source of heat they use is fossil fuels, nuclear, or geothermal, convert water – or some other fluid – into steam to drive electricity-generating turbines. The steam has to be condensed in a cooling system in order to be recycled through the turbines, and large quantities of water are also required for this purpose. Much of this water is drawn from rivers, along with lakes and aquifers and the oceans.

The energy potential of water moving in rivers has re-emerged in the modern era with the advent of hydroelectricity generation. Hydropower is the only renewable resource used on a large scale for electricity generation, and about one-third of all countries rely on hydropower for more than half their electricity. Globally, hydropower provides about 20% of the world's total electricity supply. Most large hydroelectric stations rely on a dam to supply a

8. **Cotton mills on the River Irwell in Manchester, northern England, c. 1850, where flowing water in rivers and canals was a crucial component of the Industrial Revolution**

reliable flow of water to turn their turbines, but small 'run of river' hydroelectric stations do not need such obstacles to the natural flow of the river. Countries with abundant rainfall and mountainous terrain have developed hydropower to become their foremost supply of electricity. Norway is an interesting example.

Its rivers provide more than enough hydroelectricity for its own needs so the country has become an exporter of hydropower.

Trade and transport

The flow of water in a river has always provided another obvious utility for people: as a conduit for travel, trade, and transport. Many of the world's major cities have developed on navigable rivers thanks to the access they offer, to and from their terrestrial interiors and, in many cases, to territories overseas. The River Thames and London provide a good example. In medieval England, the transportation of goods along the river played an important role in the development of London as a city, and indeed of many other settlements in the Thames valley. Water transport was attractive at this time because of its relatively low cost: moving commodities such as grain and wool by land could be more than ten times the price of transport by water. Cheap transport by river stimulated economic development by increasing the size of markets, encouraging regional specialization, and promoting urbanization. Historical research of transport along the Thames and its tributaries around the year 1300 shows that these waterways greatly extended the market for grain and fuel supplied to the capital. The specialization in farming that developed around London at this time is also likely to have been a result of the increase in transport by river, since some areas were better suited to the production of particular crops than others. Two main impacts on urban development can be identified. For London, development of the cheap fluvial transport network removed a constraint on the city's expansion because it reduced the cost of food and fuel used in the capital. Urban development was also stimulated outside London, in the capital's hinterland, as towns such as Henley-on-Thames grew to become a specialized centre supplying agricultural produce to the city.

Navigable rivers also became major arteries of trade and stimulated the growth of larger settlements elsewhere in medieval

England. Gloucester and Bristol were served by the River Severn, York had quays on the River Ouse, and Norwich on the River Wensum. The importance of water transport to urban development was even embodied in the early 12th-century Laws of Edward the Confessor, an Anglo-Saxon king of England. The laws note that navigation should be maintained on the major rivers 'along which ships transport provisions from different places to cities or burghs'.

Many economic historians suggest that England's rivers provided the cheapest form of inland transport for hefty goods right up until the 18th century. Nonetheless, bargemen and merchants wanting to use rivers for trade in the Middle Ages had to struggle constantly against those who wanted to build mills and fish-weirs. The mid-18th century is thought of as the birth of the 'canal age' in England when industrialists built their own waterways, an era that followed a 150-year period in which water transport became progressively easier as many of the country's rivers were 'improved'.

The importance of river transport has played a key role in the economic development of many countries. In Sweden, for example, in the 17th and 18th centuries, logs felled in the country's northern forests were floated down rivers to the mining district of central Sweden where they were used as fuel in smelting operations. During the second half of the 19th century, this form of river transport played an important role in the industrialization of Sweden thanks to the rapid development of an export-oriented forest industry, based on sawmills and later pulp mills. Sweden was able to supply a growing demand for sawn wood and square timber in the industrially developing economies of Western Europe from her forests in the remote northern parts of the country. Timber felling was possible over large areas of northern Sweden thanks to the country's dense network of tributaries and main rivers which generally flow from north to south, enabling cheap long-distance transport of timber to the sawmills and pulp mills on the coast. Sweden's distinctly seasonal climate was also favourable to the transport of timber, since the spring thaw swells rivers with snowmelt that facilitates the floating of logs. At the beginning of the 20th century, sawn timber, pulp, and paper accounted for about half of Sweden's exports by value. The importance of rivers in moving timber within the country only waned in the 1980s when timber-floating operations were abandoned in favour of an expanding road network.

River transport of both goods and people continues to be economically important in Bangladesh which, with some 700 rivers and major tributaries criss-crossing the country, has one of the world's largest inland waterway networks. The total length of rivers navigable by modern mechanized vessels shrinks during the dry season, but it still connects almost all the country's major cities, towns, and commercial centres. Indeed, inland ports in Bangladesh handle about 40% of the nation's foreign trade.

Inland water transport is cheaper than road or rail, and is often the only mode that serves the rural poor, proving especially useful during periods of widespread flooding in the monsoon season when many roads become impassable. Country boats, the traditional mode of river transport in Bangladesh for centuries, are also the main means of transport at any time in southern areas of the country where the road network is little developed.

In some parts of the world, trade along rivers has involved contact between radically different cultures, with a range of impacts, some beneficial, others less so. In North America, the fur trade stimulated Euro-American exploration of the Missouri River Valley in the 1700s. Native American Indians met European traders at certain points along the river, some of these trade centres pre-dating contact with Europeans by hundreds of years. American Indians provided beaver pelts and buffalo hides in exchange for manufactured and processed goods such as metal cooking pots, knives, guns, fabrics, beads, coffee, and sugar. By the

9. Several hundred thousand country boats ply the rivers of Bangladesh, moving passengers and cargo. These boats play a vital role in the lives of rural people and in the rural economy

1800s, steamboats plied up and down the Missouri River from the town of St Louis where commercial trading companies had established bases. American Indians were exposed to many aspects of Euro-American culture but also, inadvertently, to deadly diseases to which they had no immunity. One epidemic of smallpox in 1837, probably transferred to Plains Indian tribes by a steamboat passenger, killed 10,000 to 20,000 Indians, including over 90% of the Mandan Nation, proprietors of one of the Missouri River's main trading posts.

The Danube: artery of Europe

Although not its longest, many would offer the Danube as Europe's principal river, as it was in the mid-17th century when Pope Innocent X approved construction of the Four Rivers Fountain in Piazza Navona in Rome. Crowned by an Egyptian obelisk, Gian Lorenzo Bernini's most dramatic and spectacular work consists of four marble figures symbolizing the major world rivers known at the time (no doubt in part a reference to the four rivers of Eden). The Nile represented Africa, the Ganges Asia, the Rio de la Plata symbolized the Americas, and the Danube represented Europe. Linking more countries than any other river in the world, the Danube both defines and integrates the continent.

Human occupation of the Danube Valley has been traced back at least 25,000 years, when men gathered to hunt mammoth at Dolni Vestonice, in the Czech Republic of today. A natural corridor for migration linking east and west, the river was used by farmers from the Anatolian Peninsula seeking new lands to cultivate some 7,000 years ago. Five millennia later, the Persian King Darius led his vast army along the same route before crossing the Danube in his campaign against the Scythians. The river was established as a corridor for trade by the ancient Greeks and during Roman times, when the Danube was used both as a defensive barrier and as a supply line to feed and equip the legionnaires stationed along it.

Europe's Christian military forces used the Danube as a pathway for heading towards Byzantium and the Holy Land during the times of the Crusades a thousand years ago, and in the 16th century the Danube provided the route for a reverse crusade when Suleiman the Magnificent brought Islam westwards from the Black Sea. In the 1520s, the Ottoman Turks took Belgrade, defeated Hungry, and advanced to the walls of Vienna. They held Budapest for 150 years before being driven back down the Danube.

Trade along the Danube gave rise to two major empires, the Austrian and Hungarian, which merged under the Habsburgs, known to German-speakers as the *Donaumonarchie*, or 'Danube Monarchy'. Maria Theresa, archduchess of Austria and queen of Hungary and Bohemia, founded an imperial government department to oversee navigation on the river. Today, the 'prince of all European rivers', as Napoleon Bonaparte liked to call the Danube, flows through four of the continent's capital cities (Vienna, Bratislava, Budapest, and Belgrade) and through, or along the borders of, ten countries. Its role as an important artery for European trade has continued, and navigation along the entire river has been promoted since the first Danubian Commission was set up in the 19th century. The International Commission for the Protection of the Danube River, established in 1998, works to ensure the sustainable and equitable use of freshwater resources in the entire Danube Basin, including the improvement of water quality and the development of mechanisms for flood and accident control.

Given the important role played by this river throughout the history of Europe, its reflection in various aspects of European culture is not unexpected. Before Bernini's Four Rivers Fountain in Rome, the Danube had spawned a school of landscape painting in the 16th century. Some 200 years later, it became the subject of a famous musical waltz by Johann Strauss the Younger. These examples serve to illustrate some of the many ways in which rivers have presented stimulation and inspiration to writers and artists, a subject examined in more detail in the next chapter.

Chapter 4
Roads that move

Rivers are roads that move and carry us whither we wish to go.

Blaise Pascal (1623–62)
(French mathematician and philosopher)

Rivers have interested humankind for millennia. They feature
prominently in many facets of culture, providing liquid inspiration
to diverse sectors of artistic society, from poets to musicians. The
currents of a river have been harnessed not only to embody the
bucolic mysteries of nature but to carry ideas and motifs, and to
propel writers into the past. As an ever-flowing symbol of God's
work, the river combines both the spiritual and the physical, offering
an insight into humanity's place in the order of things. The long
history of the river's importance to literature and the arts stretches
from the poetry of Virgil to the celluloid of Francis Ford Coppola.

Rivers and language

The long, rich cultural relationship with rivers has many interesting
linguistic connotations. The names of numerous rivers are in
themselves descriptive. The awe-inspiring scale of flow seen in some
large rivers has simply resulted in them being called 'big' or 'mighty',
such as the Ottawa River in Canada, which derives its name from the
Algonquin word. Others are a bit more graphic. In England, the
River Thames' name is believed to come from an Indo-European

word meaning 'dark river'; the River Wellow was winding, the Swift fast-flowing, and the Cray was pure or clear. Names of Celtic origin abound in Britain: the River Dart is a Celtic river name meaning 'river where oak-trees grow', and the River Iwerne is thought to mean 'lined with yew trees'. Conversely, however, lots of rivers have names that simply mean 'river'. The Avon in the west of England gets its name from a Celtic word meaning river, so that River Avon literally means 'River River'. Similarly, the River Ganges in South Asia takes its name from the Sanskrit word *ganga*, meaning current or river.

Rivers have also had their names appropriated for use as place names. Cities named after their rivers include the capitals of Russia (Moscow: Moskva River), Lithuania (Vilnius: Vilnia River), Central African Republic (Bangui: Ubangi River), and Malawi (Lilongwe: Lilongwe River). Belmopan, the capital city of Belize, was named after two rivers: the country's longest, the Belize River, and one of its tributaries, the Mopan. On a still larger scale, a number of countries are named after their major rivers. They include Paraguay in South America, Jordan in the Middle East, Gambia and Senegal in West Africa. Further east in West Africa, the Niger River flows through both Niger and Nigeria, and Central Africa's Congo has given rise to both the Congo Republic and the Democratic Republic of the Congo. India is named after the Indus River, although it no longer flows through India. A country of sorts was created in northern Europe in 1806 by Napoleon Bonaparte when he established the Confederation of the Rhine, but it disintegrated after Napoleon's abdication in 1814.

Equally, numerous place names are linked to rivers in less direct ways. Oxford means a crossing place, or ford, used by oxen. Cambridge is traced back to 'Bridge on the River Granta' with the change from Grant-, a Celtic river name, to Cam- thought to be due to a Norman influence. Many names of settlements located at the mouth of a river have an equally simple etymology: Yarmouth and Falmouth lie at the mouths of the Rivers Yar and Fal. Of course, the same principle also applies in many other languages. Aberdeen, the port in northeast Scotland, has a name of Celtic origin ('*aber*', or mouth, of the River Don, now Deen). Similarly, Aarhus, the port in eastern Denmark, simply means 'river mouth' in Old Danish (*aa*, river, and *os*, mouth). In the USA, a number of states have names derived from Native American words associated with rivers. Connecticut comes from a Mohican word meaning 'long river place'; Mississippi is thought to mean 'great river' in Chippewa; Missouri is an Algonquin term meaning 'river of the big canoes'; and Nebraska is from an Omaha or Otos Indian word meaning 'broad water' or 'flat river'. Not all place name links to rivers are reliable, however. A good example is the Brazilian coastal city of Rio de Janeiro, named by Portuguese sailors who first discovered the spot on New Year's Day 1502. They called it 'January River', thinking – wrongly – that the large bay on which Rio now stands was the mouth of a great river.

Some terms derived from rivers have been adopted for more general use in the English language. Meander is a good example; as both verb and adjective, it has entered the vernacular to indicate a winding path. The word 'rival' – someone competing with another for the same objective – also has its origin in riverine terminology. It is derived from a Latin word, '*rivalis*', that means 'using the same stream'. The well-known phrase 'crossing the Rubicon' has its roots in history. The River Rubicon marked the boundary between two parts of the Roman Empire, and no Roman general was allowed to bring his forces south over the river because to do so was a direct challenge to the authority of Rome. Hence, when Julius Caesar decided to cross the river and march on Rome, he passed a point of no return in crossing the Rubicon.

Landscape painting

Rivers and their valleys have provided a rich source of stimulation for landscape painters in numerous parts of the world. Twisting channels wind their way through the long history of landscape painting in China. Probably the best-known painting from the Sung Dynasties, for instance, is the scroll entitled 'Along the River during the Qingming Festival' created by Zhang Zeduan in the early 12th century. Its panoramic depiction of daily life at the Sung capital, Bianjing (today's Kaifeng), is famed for its great detail of people, buildings, bridges, and boats clustered around and along the river. The painting has been mimicked by more than twenty other artists of subsequent dynasties. The most recent of these was a computer-generated animated version produced for the World Exposition in Shanghai in 2010 and shown in the Chinese Pavilion.

Some early examples of landscape painting in Europe are traced to the beginning of the 16th century, when a number of German and Austrian artists became associated with the Danube School of Landscape Painting. Based largely in the imperial city of Regensburg, their work combined Upper Italian Renaissance influences with German Gothic traditions. More than 300 years later, many of the French Impressionists drew inspiration from the transient colours and effects of light playing on the waters of the River Seine. They include Auguste Renoir, Claude Monet, Edouard Manet, and Gustave Caillebotte. Monet chose to live near the river in the village of Giverny, not far from Paris. The Seine also features in the work of later French artists, including one of Georges Seurat's best-known pointillist paintings, *A Sunday Afternoon on the Island of La Grande Jatte – 1884* (La Grande Jatte is an island in the Seine, at that time used as a bucolic retreat from the grimy centre of Paris). The Seine also provided early inspiration for the Fauvist painters Henri Matisse and Maurice de Vlaminck before they moved to the warmer climes of the Mediterranean.

Elsewhere in Europe, John Constable, the English Romantic painter of the early 19th century, is intimately associated with the River Stour particularly. Constable was born in East Bergholt, a village on the Stour in East Anglia, and the area around the river – Dedham Vale – has become known since the artist's lifetime as Constable Country. At more or less the same time, the work of the

10. *The Skiff* (*La Yole*), painted in 1875 by Pierre-Auguste Renoir. The scene is set on the River Seine, which provided a great influence for many Impressionist painters

Chernetsov brothers on the River Volga sparked a greater appreciation of landscape in Russian art (see below).

In North America, an artist named Thomas Cole made his first trip up the Hudson River to Catskill in 1825 and the paintings that resulted from this foray created a sensation in the nascent New York art world. The resulting Hudson River School lays claim to being the first coherent school of art in the USA. The group's members initially focused on panoramas along the Hudson in New York State, in celebration of the untamed landscapes, but their scope later widened to include subjects as distant as South America and the Arctic. Another US artist whose work is closely associated with a river, in this case the Mississippi, is John Banvard. In 1840, Banvard began painting large panoramas of the Mississippi which eventually culminated in a canvas some 800 metres in length (about half a mile, although it was advertised as being three miles long). Banvard put his work on display to the paying public and later took the Mississippi panorama to Europe, where he gave a private view to Queen Victoria in Windsor Castle, near London, in 1849.

The Volga: soul of Russia

Europe's longest river, the Volga, occupies a special place in the Russian psyche as a beloved symbol of national culture. Venerated in folklore, song, poetry, and painting, 'Mother River' or 'Mother Volga' represents the country's vast open spaces and embodies the lifeblood of Russia's history. The river was portrayed as a symbol of Russia in the sentimental poetry of several 19th-century writers, including Nicolai Karamzin, Ivan Dmitriev, and Nicolai Nekrasov. Prince Pyotr Viazemskii, a leading figure in the so-called Golden Age of Russian poetry during the first half of the 19th century, celebrated the Volga 'as a marker of nationality'. The lives of Volga river people were also vividly portrayed in the novels and stories of Maxim Gorky, one-time dishwasher on a Volga steamship whose early years were spent in the city of Nizhny Novgorod, at the confluence of the Volga and the River Oka.

Esteem for the Volga is a familiar focus of Russian folk songs, epitomized by the 'Song of the Volga Boatmen', a shanty traditionally sung by the river's barge-haulers who, in the era before steam, used to haul vessels along certain stretches of the river using ropes from the shore. The song was popularized by the operatic bass singer Feodor Chaliapin, himself born in the Volga region. It is intimately linked with the famous oil painting of the same name, by Ilya Repin, a striking depiction of the peasantry's terrible working conditions in Tsarist Russia, echoed in a Nekrasov poem: 'Along the river there were barge-haulers,/ and their funereal cry was unbearably wild.' Repin's work, completed in 1873, also managed to capture the dignity and fortitude of the barge-haulers, and represented a key stage in the development of the national realist school of painting. The latter half of the 19th century was a time when the river, its towns, villages, and surroundings were increasingly depicted on canvas by such celebrated Russian artists as Isaac Levitan, Ivan Shishkin, and Boris Kustidiyev. The work of Levitan particularly is known throughout Russia for its propensity to reflect the soul of Russian nature. He spent several summers on the river, and some of his best-known paintings capture the changing light, rhythm of life, and the beauty and serenity of the Volga's scenery.

Serious appreciation of the rural landscape in Russian art has been traced back to 1838, when two brothers, Grigory and Nikanor Chernetsov, were dispatched by the Ministry of the Imperial Palace under Tsar Nicholas I to travel the length of the Volga from Rybinsk to Astrakhan on a 'voyage of discovery', commissioned to draw panoramic views of 'the beautiful places on both banks of the Volga'. The result was a cyclorama some 600 metres long that was put on display in St Petersburg, in a room decorated to resemble a ship's cabin and equipped with sound effects to simulate the river journey. Sadly, the epic work did not survive the numerous unwindings of these viewings, but the Chernetsovs' journals and travel notes remain, along with some of their working sketches and oil paintings.

On film, a classic movie from the Soviet era is the musical comedy *Volga, Volga*, said to have been a favourite of the leader Joseph Stalin. The film tells the story of a talented folk singer who overcomes petty bureaucrats to travel to Moscow for a music contest and is set largely on a Volga steamboat named *The Josef Stalin*. First released in 1938, its light-hearted escapism stood in stark contrast to the economic hardships and political purges occurring in the Soviet Union at the time.

Music

Three water nymphs from the River Rhine are central characters in the monumental four-opera cycle *Der Ring des Nibelungen* (usually known in English simply as the Ring Cycle) by Richard Wagner. The Rhine maidens (nixie borrowed from Germanic folklore – see Chapter 2), are guardians of the *Rheingold*, a treasure hidden in the river which is stolen and turned into the ring at the centre of the mid-19th-century epic. They appear in the first and last scenes, eventually rising from the waters of the Rhine to reclaim the ring from the ashes of Brünnhilde's funeral pyre.

The charm and romance of the Danube is evoked in *The Waves of the Danube*, a waltz composed in 1880 by the Romanian Ion Ivanovici, but the waltz written 14 years earlier by the Austrian conductor and composer Johann Strauss the Younger is more widely acclaimed. *An der schönen blauen Donau*, better known in English as the *Blue Danube*, has been one of the most consistently popular pieces of classical music ever since.

Johann Strauss lived and worked in Vienna, then the capital of the Austro-Hungarian Empire, a centre of high culture and classical music. In Bohemia, at the time part of the empire, the Czech composer Bedrich Smetana wrote a cycle of nationalistic symphonic poems entitled *Ma vlast* (My Country), of which his portrait of the Vltava River remains the most popular piece. The musical depiction of the river's course across Bohemia flows through forests and meadows, past ruined castles and a peasant wedding, before sweeping majestically through Prague to join the River Elbe. The evocative piece cemented Smetana's position as one of the founders of the Czech nationalist movement and 'Vltava' is considered by many to be the unofficial national anthem of the Czech Republic.

The Mississippi is another river with a very strong musical tradition, particularly along its lower reaches where the river flows through that region of the USA known as the Deep South, a culturally cohesive farming area dominated by cotton plantations during the 19th and much of the 20th century. The various styles of music that originated along this part of the Mississippi have been enjoyed all over North America and beyond. The blues were created on the Mississippi Delta, the alluvial floodplains that stretch between the Mississippi and Yazoo Rivers, while further downstream the city of New Orleans gave rise to boogie-woogie and jazz. The blues became fused with gospel music to spawn rhythm and blues, rock 'n' roll, and soul music. Louis Armstrong, B. B. King, Chuck Berry, Jerry Lee Lewis, Elvis Presley, and Aretha Franklin are among the internationally renowned musicians of the 20th century born and raised on the banks of the Mississippi.

Rivers in literature

Authors and poets have used rivers in numerous ways. A river can serve not only as a geographical feature but as a literary device, its constant movement and direction giving impetus to a narrative. The river journey is one of the most common river metaphors, linking the past to the present, doubling as the journey through life, presenting insights into the experience of growing up. As a setting in fiction, the river bank offers a sense of destiny and hints at the possibility of self-discovery.

An assessment of the various ways rivers are used as poetic devices in Roman literature highlights how this vigorous and variable element of the landscape interacts with the dynamics of poetry. The river can be a mediator between poetry and poet, the flow of the river can become part of the narrative and may form part of a narrative structure. Not least in the epic *Aeneid* (19 BC) of Virgil, where the river serves as a symbol for directional progress, the journey being simultaneously spatial, temporal, and literary. The River Tiber is where Aeneas begins his travels in Italy and also provides a course for the narrative.

Another example of a river driving a poetic narrative is found in Alfred Lord Tennyson's poem *The Lady of Shalott* (1833). Everything in the poem follows the movement of the river. While the lady sits in her tower, the river reflects the world passing her by as it flows downstream to Camelot. When Sir Lancelot trots past on his horse, the lady leaves the tower and joins the reality of the river, unchaining the boat on its bank and writing her name on its prow, effectively discovering herself by establishing her identity. Her boat floats down the river to Camelot, where she dies.

Freedom, change, and metamorphosis, all qualities inherent in the course of a large river, appear clearly as themes in Mark Twain's *Huckleberry Finn* (1885), a quintessential river story set on the Mississippi. Huck Finn, the son of an abusive, alcoholic father, flees on a raft with his friend Jim, a runaway slave, down the Mississippi river. Their journey represents escape from oppression, a broken family life, racial discrimination, and social injustice, and the book draws on the author's own boyhood experiences along the Mississippi. Samuel Clemens – Twain's real name – also worked as a riverboat pilot in his twenties, an experience that gave him his pen-name, taken from a frequent call made by the man sounding the depth of the river in shallow places. Relayed to the pilot in order to keep the boat from running aground, 'mark twain' meant 'by the mark two fathoms'.

The change and renewal are more fantastical in *The Water Babies* (1863), Charles Kingsley's classic children's novel, which begins with the boy Tom, a chimney sweep, seeking a river's cleansing properties. Tom escapes his terrible life to find freedom in the river but, after his adventures as a water baby, he is finally reborn in human form once more, in a moral tale of Christian redemption. One of the most powerful works of fiction centred upon an urban river, Charles Dickens' *Our Mutual Friend* was begun the year after publication of Kingsley's novel. Published in serial form, it uses the River Thames in Victorian London to bestow rebirth and renewal upon several characters and is awash with watery imagery. The Thames is used in a similar way to change identity by William Boyd in his book *Ordinary Thunderstorms* (2009), a novel he was prompted to write by learning that the police pull a dead body from the river every week on average.

In literature, rivers are also used as agents of transformation through their representation of boundaries or thresholds, so that the practice of crossing a river precipitates some sort of change. Rivers can unify or divide, act as companion or god. Embracing the essential mysteries of nature, rivers can embody the pursuit of wisdom. They can be used to explore the physical world for our moral and intellectual, as well as physical, orientation. And of course, even within a single work, a river has many meanings.

The Congo: *Heart of Darkness*

Joseph Conrad's *Heart of Darkness* is considered by many to be the ultimate 'modernist' novel, a work of great complexity designed to reflect the complexity of experience we find in the real world. The thread running through the book, Africa's Congo River, helps to lend both direction and form to its uncertainties. The story is a simple quest, an adventurous journey upriver by one man, Marlow, in search of another, Kurtz. This is a physical journey, into a continent along a river, but also a moral and political journey, confronting the harsh realities of colonialism (Kurtz is a lost agent who works for a Belgian company involved in the ivory trade). The journey also works on another level still, becoming a psychological trip, undertaken by Marlow and the reader, in which we descend into ourselves to confront our basic drives and impulses, weaknesses and needs, a descent into the underworld that is the 'Heart of Darkness'.

The book is constructed as a tale within a tale, the narrative beginning on the estuary of the River Thames, where four men sit on the deck of a ship listening to Marlow tell his story of a trip to Africa in his youth. The setting allows the implications of what happens in the 'dark places' of a far-away continent to reverberate through the seemingly safe and comfortable world of the audience.

During Marlow's voyage upriver, an image of Kurtz gradually emerges. A man who started out as a force for good has been corrupted by the exercise of power. Kurtz has acquired a status in the local African community that is almost divine, a position consolidated by his use of force: he has plundered the countryside for its ivory, shooting people at will and displaying their skulls on his picket fence as a symbol of his authority. Marlow's journey into the heart of Africa is an exploration of the shadowy underbelly of the European Enlightenment, the language of reason, and the rhetoric of imperialism.

Conrad's *Heart of Darkness* was first published in serial form in *Blackwood's Magazine* right at the end of the 19th century, and as a book in 1902. Towards the end of the 20th century, Marlow's river trip was re-enacted in another classic of fiction, this time on celluloid, in Francis Ford Coppola's spectacular film about the

Rivers

11. Joseph Conrad immortalized the Congo in his classic modernist novel *Heart of Darkness*, a book also considered to have generated many condescending Western perceptions of sub-Saharan Africa

Vietnam War, *Apocalypse Now* (1979). The movie, although of course ostensibly set on another continent, showed that Conrad's story still had numerous contemporary echoes almost a century after its creation. Colonel Kurtz, a special forces commander driven insane by power, played by Marlon Brando, still represents the corrupted voice of Enlightenment, humanism, and supposed progress. The film, like the book, develops imagery and characters that can be interpreted as a searing criticism of war, racism, and colonialism. However, both book and film have also been viewed as expressions of the hypocritical values they are trying to expose.

Coppola's film also came with a tale within a tale, simultaneously generating the documentary film *Hearts of Darkness*, a record of the making of *Apocalypse Now* that was a testimony to real-life corruption, decadence, and insanity worthy of the fictional Kurtz. In all cases – the book, the film, and the film about the film – the story is told only from the perspective of the outsiders. No effort is made to understand the alien continent through which the river flows. This can be criticized as emblematic of Europe's mythologizing of Africa in general, and of the Congo in particular, and of the USA's blinkered crusade for freedom and democracy. But this lack of an alternative frame of reference is also essential to the multi-faceted objectives of each story. Each is intended to be an essentially solitary journey involving profound spiritual change in the voyager, a mission to the very centre of things that cannot find simple answers to the questions of human existence. Kurtz's character remains as enigmatic as the darkness in which he has taken up residence. In each case, the river plays a pivotal role, in Conrad's words, as a conduit for the 'dreams of men' and the 'germs of empires'.

Chapter 5
Tamed rivers

> The servitude of rivers is the noblest and most important victory
> which man has obtained over the licentiousness of nature.
>
> Edward Gibbon (1737–94)
> (English historian)

People have interacted with rivers throughout human history and
their impacts, both direct and indirect, have taken many forms.
The earliest examples of water being extracted from rivers on a
significant scale for the irrigation of crops date back 6,000 years.
Deliberate manipulation of river channels through engineering
works, including dam construction, diversion, channelization, and
culverting, also has a long history. Some of the world's oldest
dams, in the Middle East, were built more than 4,500 years ago
and deliberate diversion and regulation of the Yellow River in
China, for example, began more than 2,000 years before the
present. Since these early examples, the deliberate human
alteration of rivers all over the world has expanded in its extent
and escalated in its ambition and scale. Nevertheless, significant
geographical differences in the degree and intensity of river
modifications remain. In Europe today, almost 80% of the total
discharge of the continent's major rivers is affected by measures
designed to regulate flow, whether for drinking water supply,
hydroelectric power generation, flood control, or any other reason.
The proportion in individual countries is higher still. About 90%

12. Rivers in even the most inaccessible regions are affected to some extent by human activities, as here in the Darien Gap in Panama, an area renowned globally for its remoteness

of rivers in the UK are regulated as a result of these activities, while in the Netherlands this percentage is close to 100. By contrast, some of the largest rivers on other continents, including the Amazon and the Congo, are hardly manipulated at all.

Direct and intentional modifications to rivers are complemented by the impacts of land use and land use changes which frequently result in the alteration of rivers as an unintended side effect. Deforestation, afforestation, land drainage, agriculture, and the use of fire have all had significant impacts, with perhaps the most extreme effects produced by construction activity and urbanization. These impacts are diverse and are not all direct. Many aspects of a dynamic river channel and its associated ecosystems are mutually adjusting, so a human activity in a landscape that affects the supply of water or sediment is likely to set off a complex cascade of other alterations. When contemporary climate change is included in the vast array of human activities that in some way result in changes to rivers, many authorities argue that few, if any, rivers – even in the world's least populated regions – remain unaffected by human impact. In many ways, therefore, the evolution and development of rivers is driven as much by social and economic factors as by natural ones.

Irrigated agriculture

One of the most important developments in human society was the shift from a subsistence way of life based on hunting and gathering food from the wild to one primarily based on food production derived from cultivated plants and domesticated animals. The links between early agricultural management and the emergence of urban civilizations in just a few independent centres around the world have been noted in Chapter 3 along the alluvial valleys of the Tigris-Euphrates, the Nile, and the Indus. These links developed from the high levels of organization needed to manage permanent agricultural fields and systems of irrigation. Another centre of early crop irrigation using river water was in the Zaña Valley on the western slopes of the Peruvian Andes, where archeologists have unearthed a system of small-scale gravity canals that were being used at least 5,400 years ago, and probably 6,500 years ago.

Irrigated agriculture is arguably just as important today as it was to those early civilizations, and although several sources of fresh water are used to irrigate cropland – including groundwater, lakes, direct runoff, and various forms of wastewater – rivers remain by far the most important. The methods of storage (in reservoirs) and distribution (by canal) have not changed fundamentally since the earliest river irrigation schemes, with the exception of some contemporary projects' use of pumps to distribute water over greater distances. Nevertheless, many irrigation canals still harness the force of gravity. Half the world's large dams (defined as being 15 metres or higher) were built exclusively or primarily for irrigation, and about one-third of the world's irrigated cropland relies on reservoir water. In several countries, including such populous nations as India and China, more than 50% of arable land is irrigated by river water supplied from dams.

The knock-on effects of withdrawing water from a river to irrigate crops can be striking. In some cases, it may induce a complete transformation of river dimensions, pattern, and shape. One example of such 'river metamorphosis' comes from the western Great Plains of the USA, where rivers described by European Americans towards the end of the 19th century as wide, shallow, braided channels with only sparse vegetation along their banks have since been altered dramatically. The regulation of river flow for irrigated agriculture resulted in lower seasonal peak flows, higher base flows, and a change in regional water tables that promoted the establishment of trees along river banks. The combination of these changes to flow regime and bank resistance resulted in the rivers becoming narrow, sinuous channels flanked by dense forests within just a few decades.

Sadly, many irrigation schemes are not well managed and a number of environmental problems are frequently experienced as a result, both on-site and off-site. In many large networks of irrigation canals, less than half of the water diverted from a river or reservoir actually benefits crops. A lot of water seeps away through unlined canals or evaporates before reaching the fields. Some also runs off the fields or infiltrates through the soil, unused by plants, because farmers apply too much water or at the wrong time. Much of this water seeps back into nearby streams or joins underground aquifers, so can be used again, but the quality of water may deteriorate if it picks up salts, fertilizers, or pesticides. Excessive applications of irrigation water often result in rising water tables beneath fields, causing salinization and waterlogging. These processes reduce crop yields on irrigation schemes all over the world.

Many of these difficulties have plagued farmers in the Central Asian states of Turkmenistan and Uzbekistan where desert conditions mean that more than 90% of agriculture relies on irrigation from the Amu Darya and Syr Darya rivers. A rapid expansion of irrigation in Central Asia was initiated in the 1950s during the Soviet era, with some dramatic consequences. By the 1980s, the irrigated area had more than doubled to occupy about 7 million hectares. As a result, the annual inflow to the Aral Sea from the two rivers, the source of 90% of its water, had declined by an order of magnitude from about 55 cubic kilometres a year to some 5 cubic kilometres annually.

Unsurprisingly, the Aral Sea has become considerably smaller in consequence. In 1960, it was the fourth largest lake in the world, but since that time its surface area has more than halved, it has lost two-thirds of its volume, and its water level has dropped by more than 25 metres. In some areas, the Aral Sea's remaining waters are more than twice as salty as sea water in the open ocean. Most of the lake's native fish and other aquatic species have disappeared, unable to survive in the salt water, meaning an end to a once-major commercial fishing industry. Receding sea levels have also had local effects on climate, and the exposed sea bed has become a source of major dust storms that billow out over surrounding agricultural land up to several hundred kilometres from the Aral's coastline. This fine dust is laden with salts, adding to the problems of irrigated agriculture. It is also thought to have damaging impacts on human health.

Effects on fish

People have directly affected the biology of rivers over a very long period. In Europe, the common carp is found in the rivers of every country, but the fish is native only to the Danube and some of its tributaries. It was introduced to many European rivers by the Romans about 2,000 years ago after large numbers of legionnaires developed a taste for wild carp while stationed along the Danube – then the northern boundary of the Roman Empire – in the province of Pannonia.

This was how the common carp became the first species to be introduced into the Seine in France, for instance. It was followed in the Middle Ages by other species, including tench and rudd, which escaped from fish-farming ponds kept by noblemen and religious communities. In the late 19th century, further invaders (nase and pikeperch) arrived in the Seine from rivers further east via canals. These were followed at the end of the century by deliberate introductions of North American species: rainbow trout, black bass, pumpkinseed, and black bullhead.

Native fish began to disappear from the Seine in the 20th century as the construction of weirs and locks made it impossible for migratory species to reach their upstream spawning grounds. With the exception of the eel, all of the Seine's migratory species became extinct: sturgeon, salmon, sea lamprey, sea trout, European smelt, and shad. The original fish fauna of the Seine probably consisted of about 30 species. Today, the river has 46 species, but only 24 of them are native.

The catalogue of human impacts on the fish biology of the Seine is fairly typical of many rivers in the more economically developed parts of the world. Biological invasions generally are widely acknowledged to be one of the major threats to biodiversity across the world in rivers as well as other ecosystems. A study of the global patterns of freshwater fish invasions in more than 1,000 river basins covering more than 80% of the Earth's continental surface identified western and southern Europe as one of six global invasion hotspots, where non-native species represent more than one-quarter of the total number of species per basin. These hotspots also have the highest proportion of threatened fish species.

The human impact was found to be the most important determinant of this situation, particularly the level of economic activity, expressed by the gross domestic product, in a given river basin. The pattern can probably be explained in several ways. Regions that are economically prosperous are more prone to habitat disturbances (e.g. dams and reservoirs modifying river flows) that are known to assist the establishment of non-native species. High rates of economic activity are also likely to increase the chances of invading species arriving via aquaculture, sport fishing, and the ornamental trade. A higher demand for imported products associated with economic development also increases the likelihood of unintentional introductions occurring when imports are made.

Multiple human impacts also contribute to ecological change in rivers in poorer parts of the world, of course. Madagascar, like many islands, has a great many 'endemic' species (those found nowhere else) of all sorts, including fish, and its freshwater species are considered extremely vulnerable. Four of Madagascar's 64 endemic freshwater fish species are feared extinct, and another 38 are endangered due to three main pressures: habitat degradation caused by deforestation, overfishing, and interactions with exotic species.

Madagascar's widespread deforestation has contributed to the degradation of aquatic habitats in numerous ways. The loss of trees along river banks can result in changes in the species found in the river because fewer trees means a decline in plant matter and insects falling from them, items eaten by some fish. Fewer trees on river banks also results in less shade. More sunlight reaching the river results in warmer water and the enhanced growth of algae. A change in species can occur as fish that feed on falling food are edged out by those able to feed on algae. Deforestation also typically results in more runoff and more soil erosion. This sediment may cover spawning grounds, leading to lower reproduction rates. More sediment can also clog the gills of fish, causing them greater stress which, in combination with other pressures, can lead to their demise.

Overfishing of freshwater species is an intractable problem given the rising demand for fish from a rapidly increasing human population in Madagascar and the great logistical difficulties faced in enforcing any sort of environmental regulations. Exotic fish species introduced to the island include both aquacultural and ornamental species, and their impact on aquatic ecosystems has been profound. Some exotics have become naturalized, completely replacing native fish in the central highlands of Madagascar and becoming widespread in other parts of the island.

River regulation

Efforts to control the water level of rivers and the variability of river flows, to meet the demands of society, date back to the earliest civilizations. Today, rivers are regulated for many reasons, primarily to maintain an even flow for domestic, agricultural, and industrial needs, for hydroelectric power generation, for navigation, and to prevent flooding. The major methods employed in river regulation are the construction of large dams (see below), the building of run-of-river impoundments such as weirs and locks, and by channelization, a term that covers a range of river engineering works including widening, deepening, straightening, and the stabilization of banks.

13. The lower reaches of the West Lyn River flowing through Lynmouth in southwestern England were channelized after a devastating flood that killed 34 people in the village in 1952. The channel was widened and embankments built to increase its capacity

Some of the earliest scientific principles of channel regulation were established in Italy, where Leonardo da Vinci is credited with the invention of the pound lock using built-in vertical gates as a means of overcoming variations in river level. He produced the design at the end of the 15th century for a lock on the Naviglio Grande canal from Ticino to Milan, a development that acted as a considerable spur to inland navigation. Two hundred years later, the 'science of waters' was well established in northern Italy with the creation of a chair of 'hydrometry' at the University of Bologna in 1694 and publication of a host of books on river hydraulics. At this time it was advocated that regulation of braided rivers was best achieved by reducing them to a single channel, and by the end of the 19th century most braided rivers in western Europe had been regulated in this way.

Another important phase of river engineering that took place in Europe during the 19th century was the widespread straightening of channels and deepening of beds on major rivers. Significant work of this nature was conducted on the Seine in France and on the Sulina branch of the Danube delta, but one of the most dramatic schemes was implemented on the Tisza River, a tributary of the Danube that flows through Hungary. Regulation of the Tisza, designed to drain land for agriculture and reduce flooding on the Hungarian plain, involved cutting off more than 100 meanders, thus shortening the length of the river by nearly 400 kilometres.

The Yellow: 'China's Sorrow'

One of the most remarkable case histories of river management has unfolded over many centuries along the Yellow River, or Huanghe. It is the world's fourth longest river, although it is only number two in China after the Yangtze, and is also regarded as the world's siltiest, deriving its name from the 1.6 billion tonnes of fine yellow sediment it carries each year as it flows out of the Loess Plateau region and enters the North China Plain. The Yellow

River originates on the Tibetan Plateau and flows for more than 5,000 kilometres to the Bohai Sea, an inlet of the North Pacific Ocean. But it hasn't always done so. Like many rivers, the Yellow has changed its course over the years, albeit more frequently than most. In fact, over about the last 2,500 years, the Yellow River has averaged a major change in its course roughly every century. On some occasions, it has not flowed into the Bohai Sea, diverting into the Yellow Sea more than 300 kilometres to the south. For several hundred years, it didn't flow into the sea at all, but into a lake.

Every channel change has meant a major flood disaster on the densely populated plains of eastern China. Indeed, the Yellow's propensity to flood has earned it the nick-name of 'China's Sorrow'. One flood near the sizable city of Kaifeng in September 1642 drowned an estimated 340,000 people, leaving Kaifeng with a population of just 30,000 inhabitants. The Chinese began trying to prevent such floods more than 2,200 years ago by building up the Yellow's river banks with dykes or levées. At the beginning of the 21st century, levées lined the last 870 kilometres of the lower Yellow River to the sea. Constructing levées has probably saved many lives, but the banks have failed in numerous places over the years, still causing inundation on a catastrophic scale.

One of these levée failures, in 1938, was deliberate. During the war against the Japanese, the Chinese Nationalist government ordered its army to dynamite the levée at Huayuankou in an attempt to stop the advance of Japanese forces with an intentional flood. Although several thousand Japanese troops were drowned, the flood only delayed the enemy advance. The brunt of the disaster was borne by the local Chinese population. Eleven cities and more than 4,000 villages were inundated. In total, about 12 million people were affected, nearly 900,000 of them drowning. It was nine years before engineers repaired the levée at Huayuankou and the river resumed its course to the Bohai Sea.

Centuries of levée construction have had other effects. Most rivers in their lower courses deposit mud and silt, and the Yellow is no exception. However, because the river floods only rarely in its lower course, thanks to the levées, most of the material is deposited on the bed of the channel itself. Hence, the river channel has slowly gained height over the centuries, and the levées have had to be raised accordingly. Today, the bed of the lower reaches is on average some 5 metres higher than the land outside its dykes. At Kaifeng, the river bed is 13 metres higher than street level. The residents of Xinxiang go about their business no less than 20 metres below the adjacent Yellow River. The phenomenon is often referred to as a 'hanging river'.

Since the 1960s, a number of large dams and reservoirs have been built in the upper and middle reaches of the Yellow River. They are designed both to help control floods and to supply the 100 million people who rely on the river for their fresh water. The rising demands on the Yellow River's water have created a scarcity, to the extent that in the early 1990s the river failed to reach the sea on certain days. By 1997, there were 226 'no-flow' days, the dry point starting 700 kilometres inland on some occasions. Since then, the Chinese government has ensured for political reasons that the river always reaches the sea, albeit in small volumes. But the river now certainly delivers much less than a billion tonnes of sediment a year to the North Pacific. With so little water actually flowing in the hanging part of the river, the chances of a flood have decreased, but the possibility remains that a major flood further upstream will be too great for the dams to contain and the levées on the lower Yellow will once again be breached, with terrible consequences.

Dams

One of the most profound ways in which people alter rivers is by damming them. Obstructing a river and controlling its flow in this way brings about a raft of changes. A dam traps sediments and nutrients, alters the river's temperature and chemistry, and affects the processes of erosion and deposition by which the river sculpts the landscape. Dams create more uniform flow in rivers, usually by reducing peak flows and increasing minimum flows. Since the natural variability in flow is important for river ecosystems and their biodiversity, when dams even out flows the result is commonly fewer fish of fewer species.

Although dams have been built on rivers for thousands of years, the past 50 years or so has seen a marked escalation in the rate and scale of construction of dams all over the world, thanks to advances in earth-moving and concrete technology. At the beginning of the 21st century, there were about 800,000 dams worldwide, some towering more than 200 metres in height. Certain rivers have been intensively manipulated in this way. North America's River Columbia, for example, has, since the mid-19th century, become the site for no fewer than 80 dams. In some large river systems, the capacity of dams is sufficient to hold more than the entire annual average discharge of the river. The reservoirs behind dams on the Volta River in West Africa can store more than four times the river's annual average flow. Globally, the world's major reservoirs are thought to control about 15% of all runoff from the land. The volume of water trapped worldwide in reservoirs of all sizes is no less than five times the total global annual river flow, and this huge redistribution of water is thought to be responsible for a very small but measurable change in the orbital characteristics of the Earth.

The very first dams were constructed to control floods and to supply water for crop irrigation and domestic use. Modern dams still provide these services, plus a number of others, including hydroelectricity generation and industrial water supply. There is no doubt that many dam schemes have been very successful in achieving their objectives, and in many respects have made substantial contributions to the sustainable use of river resources. In Egypt, the Aswan High Dam has been perceived as a great symbol of economic advancement and national prestige since its completion in 1970. It generates about 20% of the country's electricity, and water held in its reservoir, Lake Nasser, has enabled irrigated agriculture to expand on to 5,000 square kilometres of new land. This is particularly important for a desert country with only a very small area suitable for cultivation. The creation of Lake Nasser has also given rise to a new fishing industry. The dam allows management of the highly seasonal variations in discharge, evening out the Nile's flow to protect against both floods and droughts. The stability of water levels in the river's course has also brought benefits for navigation and tourism.

Despite the success of many dams in achieving their main aims, however, their construction and the creation of an associated reservoir bring about significant environmental changes, many of which have proved to be detrimental. The precise nature and magnitude of changes vary greatly with the type of reservoir and the way it is operated, as well as according to the nature of the river basin affected. The most obvious impact of a new dam is the inundation of an area for its reservoir, with associated effects on hydrology, vegetation, wildlife, local climate, and even tectonic processes.

Reservoirs formed by river impoundment typically undergo significant variations in water quality during their first decade or so, before a new ecological balance is reached. Biological production can be high on initial impoundment, due to the release of organically bound elements from flooded vegetation and soils, but declines thereafter. One effect of the nutrient enrichment typical of new reservoirs, particularly in tropical and sub-tropical regions, is the blooming of toxic microscopic algae known as cyanobacteria. These cyanobacterial toxins are dangerous to humans and animals if consumed in sufficient quantities, causing a range of gastrointestinal and allergenic illnesses. Another biological consequence of large reservoirs is the rapid spread of waterweeds that cause hazards to navigation and a number of secondary

14. The Warragamba Dam near Sydney, Australia, is one of the world's largest domestic water supply dams. Its reservoir, which is 52 kilometres long, provides 80% of the water for about 4 million people in the Sydney region

impacts, notably the loss of water through evapotranspiration. A dramatic example occurred on the Brokopondo reservoir in Surinam during its first two years, where water hyacinth quickly proliferated to cover about half the lake's surface.

Some reservoirs are very large: Brokopondo covers an area of about 1,500 square kilometres, but Lake Volta, the reservoir behind the Akosombo Dam in Ghana, is more than five times as big, making it the world's largest man-made lake. The creation of such vast new bodies of water is thought to affect local climates. Following the establishment of Lake Volta, the peak rainfall season in central Ghana has shifted from October to July/August. Some particularly deep reservoirs can trigger earthquakes due to the stress on crustal rocks induced by huge volumes of water. Nurek Dam on the Vakhish River in central Tajikistan is one of the best-documented examples of a large dam causing seismic activity. This part of Central Asia is tectonically active anyway, but initial filling of the reservoir and each period of substantial increase in water level was mirrored by significant increases in earthquake frequency during the first decade of the dam's lifetime.

The building of a new dam means that any previous inhabitants of the area designated for the reservoir must be moved. The numbers of people involved can be very large and some of the biggest schemes in this respect have been in China. The Sanmen Gorge Project on the Yellow River involved resettling 300,000 people, and the Three Gorges Dam on the Yangtze River has displaced about 1.2 million people from 13 cities, 140 towns, and more than 1,000 villages. Governments usually offer compensation to people who are displaced by a new reservoir, but in many remote areas inhabitants do not possess formal ownership documents for the land they live on, a problem that can slow or actually prevent legal compensation.

Downstream of a reservoir, the hydrological regime of a river is modified. Discharge, velocity, water quality, and thermal characteristics are all affected, leading to changes in the channel and its landscape, plants, and animals, both on the river itself and in deltas, estuaries, and offshore. By slowing the flow of river water, a dam acts as a trap for sediment and hence reduces loads in the river downstream. As a result, the flow downstream of the dam is highly erosive. A relative lack of silt arriving at a river's delta can result in more coastal erosion and the intrusion of seawater that brings salt into delta ecosystems. Downstream changes in salinity due to construction of the Cahora Bassa Dam in Mozambique threaten mangrove forests at the mouth of the River Zambezi. One knock-on effect of this is a decline in prawns and shrimps, both of which breed in mangroves.

The most dramatic downstream effects have occurred on rivers dammed in several places. Construction of a series of dams in the 20th century on the Colorado River, one of the most intensively used waterways in the USA, has severely cut the river's naturally heavy sediment load, which had led the Spanish explorer Francisco Garces to name it (Rio Colorado is Spanish for 'red-coloured river'). Before 1930, the river carried more than 100 million tonnes of sediment suspended in its water each year to the delta of the Gulf of California, but it delivered neither sediment nor water to the sea from 1964, when Glen Canyon Dam was completed, to 1981, when Lake Powell behind the dam was filled to capacity for the first time. Since then, river water has reached the Gulf of California only irregularly, when discharges from dams allow. On average, the river now delivers an annual sediment load to the Gulf of California that is three orders of magnitude smaller than the pre-1930 average. The decline in fresh water and nutrients brought by the river to its estuary and the Gulf of California has had a huge impact on ecology. One study suggests that the lack of river-borne nutrients today may have resulted in a 96% decrease in the population of shellfish in the Colorado River Delta in Mexico.

The effects of dams on river ecology are numerous. Other important drivers of ecological impacts include changes in river temperature, the amount of dissolved oxygen carried, and the barrier effect of dams on the dispersal and migration of plants and animals. The dam-barrier effect on migratory fish and their access to spawning grounds has been recognized in Europe since medieval times. A statute introduced in Scotland in 1214 required all dams to be fitted with an opening and all barrier nets to be lifted every Saturday to allow salmon to pass. The problem certainly continues, however, sometimes with considerable economic implications. For example, a dramatic decline in catches of Caspian Sea sturgeon, the source of caviar, during the late 20th century was attributable primarily to the construction of several large hydroelectric dams on the River Volga and the consequent loss of spawning grounds.

Disruption to the movements of fish is one of several reasons for a recent movement in some countries to decommission dams. The small number of dams removed includes those that no longer serve a useful purpose, are too expensive to maintain, or have levels of environmental impact now deemed unacceptable. Most dams that have been removed or considered for removal are on rivers in the USA, but several European countries have also been involved in dam decommissioning. For example, two dams were destroyed and the debris cleared from tributaries of the Loire River in France in 1998 as part of a long-term government management scheme – the Plan Loire Grandeur Nature – for the river and its basin. A central aim of the scheme is to ensure the environmental protection of the Loire and to restore the river's salmon population. Removal of the Maisons-Rouges Dam on the River Vienne and the Saint Etienne de Vigan Dam on the River Allier was designed to restore access to salmon spawning grounds.

Land use

Rivers are intimately connected to the landscapes through which they flow, so it should come as no surprise to learn that any changes in a landscape inevitably affect its rivers. The way people use landscapes strongly influences rivers in numerous ways at multiple scales. Clearing natural forest vegetation to provide land for cultivation, for example, is well known to cause less interception of rainfall, less infiltration of water into the soil, less evapotranspiration, and more surface runoff, typically causing enhanced rates of soil erosion, in some cases by several orders of magnitude. Much of that soil finds its way into a river, causing associated changes in channel form and ecology. These types of alteration to rivers have been recorded all over the world, first occurring thousands of years ago in agricultural areas of the Mediterranean and China, and more recently elsewhere. Other forms of food production can also increase runoff and erosion. Grazing and trampling by livestock reduces vegetation cover and causes the compaction of soil, which reduces its infiltration capacity.

As rainwater passes over or through the soil in areas of intensive agriculture, it picks up residues from pesticides and fertilizers and transports them to rivers. In this way, agriculture has become a leading source of river pollution in certain parts of the world. Concentrations of nitrates and phosphates, derived from fertilizers, have risen notably in many rivers in Europe and North America since the 1950s and have led to a range of environmental, social, and economic problems encompassed under the term 'eutrophication' – the raising of biological productivity caused by nutrient enrichment. The growth of algae is the primary concern, leading to human health problems – and hence additional costs of water treatment for drinking – and effects on other river species. In slow-moving rivers, for example, the growth of algae reduces light penetration and depletes the oxygen content of the water, sometimes causing fish kills.

Of course, many of these effects can be controlled by conscious efforts to conserve soil and water on agricultural land. These sorts of measures are undertaken for all sorts of reasons, not least because losing soil and water from fields has an adverse effect on crop yields. Numerous studies undertaken in the Yellow River Basin in China have demonstrated the benefits of soil and water conservation measures, including tree planting and the construction of terraces, introduced in this area primarily to reduce sedimentation in the river's reservoirs. Discontinuing a land use that exacerbates runoff or sediment production is also likely to reduce these effects if the previous vegetation cover is re-established, but this does not always occur. Investigations in the central Andes of Peru found that where agricultural terraces had been abandoned, the rates of soil erosion increased because the environment was too dry for plants to grow on the terraces without attention from farmers.

Another form of land use that has similar effects is mining. In western Siberia, the sediment load of the Kolyma River more than doubled during the 1970s and 1980s due to widespread gold mining in the catchment disturbing vegetation and increasing erosion. Interestingly, records of the Kolyma's discharge over the same period showed no significant trend, indicating that runoff had remained the same. Many mining operations have also caused contamination in rivers. Waste rock and 'tailings' – the impurities left after a mineral is extracted from its ore – typically still contain metals which can be leached into soils and waterways. The accidental release of polluted water from a pond at the Aznalcóllar pyrite mine in southwest Spain in 1998 caused huge damage to birds, fish, and other aquatic species in the Guadiamar River and the Coto Doñana wetland. The water was acidic and contained arsenic, lead, and zinc at concentrations that were lethal for wildlife. Mining has long been associated with impacts on rivers. The Romans developed techniques of hydraulic mining, diverting large volumes of river water to break up and flush away soil and rock and expose minerals. The techniques were widely used to produce gold from alluvial deposits in northwest Spain.

The innumerable links between a river and human activities in its surrounding landscape, and consequently the importance of managing an entire basin, have been recognized for centuries. In Japan, for example, government regulation of timber harvesting along mountain streams in order to maintain channel stability dates back 1,200 years. Similarly, the traditional Hawaiian systems of *ahupua'a* involved managing drainage basins as an integrated whole to safeguard food production from agriculture and fish ponds. Upland forests were protected by taboo in order to supply rivers with nutrients for downstream fields and fish ponds. In modern parlance, the approach is embodied in 'catchment management plans' which in the countries of the European Union have become mandatory for all major river basins.

The Mississippi

The Mississippi River which, together with the Missouri River, drains two-thirds of the continental USA, has been significantly modified by numerous human activities over the last 200 years or so. A rapid rise in river traffic dating from the beginning of steam boats in the early 1800s spurred the large-scale felling of forests to fire the boats' boilers, and the loss of trees in turn destabilized river banks and contributed to unpredictable migration of the channel. Deforestation and the expansion of commercial agriculture in the Mississippi Basin also resulted in more soil erosion and more sediment reaching the river. Sandbars, a menace to navigation, were one result. As settlements expanded on to low-lying river banks, the Mississippi's floods became a greater danger.

Attempts to manage these problems on the Mississippi in a systematic way began in the 19th century and continue today. Throughout the 1800s, the US Army Corps of Engineers cleared rock and made the channel deeper on particular stretches of the river in an effort to assist navigation. A major programme of river engineering was initiated after a disastrous flood in 1927 in the Lower Mississippi Valley which cost more than 200 lives and displaced over 600,000 people. The Mississippi River and

15. Maintaining the Mississippi's role as an important transport route has been the motivation for many human impacts on the river. This barge is near Baton Rouge, Louisiana, where the channel is about 700 metres wide

Tributaries Project was designed to control flooding and improve navigation in several ways, and one of these was to straighten the channel by eliminating meanders. Artificially creating a meander cut-off shortens the course of the river, so increasing its gradient and speed of flow. In this way, the water erodes and deepens the channel, thereby increasing its flood capacity. The huge scale of this operation was reflected in a dramatic shortening of the Mississippi. In 1929, a boat sailing between Memphis, Tennessee, and Red River Landing in Louisiana travelled 885 kilometres, but by 1942 the same journey had been shortened by 274 kilometres – some 30% – thanks to the series of cut-offs.

Further protection from floods is provided by nearly 3,500 kilometres of levées and floodwalls along the Mississippi River itself and along some of its major tributaries, but despite these huge efforts the Mississippi is still prone to flooding. The 1993 flood on the river's upper reaches ranks as one of the worst natural disasters in US history, destroying or seriously damaging more than 40,000 buildings. Heavy rain caused the river to breach the levées in more than 1,000 places, and in many locations flooding was prolonged because levées prevented the return of water to the channel once the peak had passed. It also seems very likely that efforts to manage the flood hazard on the Mississippi have contributed to an increased risk of damage from tropical storms on the Gulf of Mexico coast. The levées built along the river have contributed to the loss of coastal wetlands, starving them of sediment and fresh water, thereby reducing their dampening effect on storm surge levels. This probably enhanced the damage from Hurricane Katrina which struck the city of New Orleans in 2005.

Urban rivers

Cities have had numerous impacts on rivers, starting with the rise of the first urban civilizations which emerged on the floodplains of large rivers in several parts of the world a few thousand years ago (see Chapter 3). Archaeological excavations at Harappa and Mohenjo Daro in the Indus Valley have revealed ceramic pipes designed to supply water and brick conduits under the streets for drainage that are thought to have been in operation 5,000 years ago. The Romans are also well known for their sophisticated water-supply systems. Water was brought to Ancient Rome from distant streams and springs via nine major aqueducts. Some of these were more than 60 kilometres in length and involved tunnelling through difficult hillsides with vertical shafts dug for inspection and cleaning.

Large amounts of water were involved in these early municipal systems, but they were ultimately limited in the volume of water managed by the force of gravity. Water could be transferred from one place to another only as long as the direction was down a slope. Modern civilization has hugely increased its ability to move water by using energy to pump water. In the southwestern USA, for example, water from the Colorado River is pumped nearly 500 kilometres across the Mojave Desert to large cities on the west coast of California, including Los Angeles and San Diego.

The growth and development of urban areas – the process of urbanization – is frequently associated with such changes to river systems, some deliberate, others inadvertent. Deliberate manipulation of rivers can be on a significant scale. In Japan, for instance, the city of Tokyo began to develop rapidly after the mid-17th century realization of the Tone River Easterly Diversion Project, a grand scheme that took more than 50 years to complete and involved diverting the Tone River more than 100 kilometres to the east to prevent flooding of the nascent city. The early stages of urban development typically result in a number of other, more subtle effects on rivers. Trees and other vegetation are removed prior to construction which results in less interception of rainfall and less transpiration, both leading to a greater flow of water and more erosion of the bare surfaces, often leading to sedimentation within river channels. In places where scientists have monitored soil erosion from construction sites, the yield of sediment has been up to 100 times greater than under natural conditions. In one extreme case, a rate of more than 600,000 tonnes of soil a year was measured from an abandoned construction site in Kuala Lumpur in Malaysia, about 20,000 times the natural erosion rate.

Other impacts in the early stages of urban development stem from growing numbers of people drawing water directly from a river or drilling wells which can indirectly affect river hydrology by lowering the water table. Rivers also provide a ready source of modern construction materials, and the excavation of sand and gravel can have significant impacts on the geometry and ecology of a river.

One of the most important effects cities have on rivers is the way in which urbanization affects flood runoff. Large areas of cities are typically impermeable, being covered by concrete, stone, tarmac, and bitumen. This tends to increase the amount of runoff produced in urban areas, an effect exacerbated by networks of storm drains and sewers. This water carries relatively little sediment (again, because soil surfaces have been covered by impermeable materials), so when it reaches a river channel it typically causes erosion and widening. Larger and more frequent floods are another outcome of the increase in runoff generated by urban areas.

Contamination of river water has always been an issue in large urban areas, but particularly serious water pollution problems occurred with the growth of cities during the Industrial Revolution thanks to large volumes of domestic sewage and industrial effluents. Water quality in the River Thames at London declined throughout the first half of the 19th century as the city's population grew, along with a rapid increase in the use of the flushing water closet. Untreated sewage flowed directly into the river, along with liquid wastes from a growing number of factories, slaughter houses, tanneries, and other industries located on the Thames.

Organic liquid wastes such as sewage and effluent from industries that process agricultural products can be broken down by bacteria and other micro-organisms in the presence of oxygen. An overload of such organic wastes leads to decreasing levels of dissolved oxygen in a river, so that fish and aquatic plant life suffer and may eventually die. By 1849, fish had disappeared from the tidal Thames, which included the entire length of the river in London. At this time, river water was still being abstracted for public consumption and water-related diseases were rife: five cholera epidemics occurred in London between 1830 and 1871. During the long, dry summer of 1858, the so-called Year of the Great Stink, the Houses of Parliament had to be abandoned on some days because of the terrible stench from the river.

Such a direct impact on the nation's politicians produced some positive action, and conditions in the Thames had improved by the 1890s with the introduction of sewage treatment plants. During the first half of the 20th century, however, sewage treatment and storage did not keep pace with London's growing population, and the oxygen content of the river reached zero 20 kilometres downstream of London Bridge during many summers. Water quality gradually improved after 1950 with tighter controls on effluent and improved treatment facilities. By the 1970s, the river's water was widely regarded as satisfactory, and in 1974 much publicity accompanied the landing of the first salmon caught in the Thames since 1833.

A similar story can be told for rivers flowing through major cities in many parts of the industrialized world: a rapid increase in pollution that accompanies industrialization and population growth leading, in time, to the implementation of pollution controls and recovery to a tolerable environmental quality. Some of the early 21st century's most polluted urban rivers are in the rapidly industrializing parts of Asia. They include the Buriganga River in Dhaka, Bangladesh; the Marilao River in Metro Manila, in the Philippines; the Citarum River near Jakarta, Indonesia; and the Yangtze River which flows through numerous cities in China.

Controlling river blindness

Flooding is the most widespread hazard to human society associated with rivers, but in certain parts of the world a disease named onchocerciasis, or river blindness, is a more enduring concern. The disease is caused by a parasitical worm that is transmitted among humans by the bites of small black flies which breed in rapid-flowing rivers and streams. Once inside the human body, the worms form disfiguring nodules on the skin and their tiny larvae move, causing blindness if they reach the eye. The World Health Organization estimates that more than 17 million people are infected worldwide, some half a million of whom are visually impaired.

River blindness occurs in parts of tropical Africa, Latin America, and the Arabian peninsula. The presence of the parasite in Latin America is almost certainly a result of infected people moving to the Americas, probably as part of the slave trade. The highest prevalence and the most serious manifestations of the disease still occur in West Africa despite the significant success of a huge programme initiated in the early 1970s to control the disease. The Onchocerciasis Control Programme in West Africa focused on controlling the black fly that transmits the disease by spraying vast stretches of West African rivers with insecticide. At the peak of the programme, this involved more than 50,000 kilometres of river over an area of more than a million square kilometres in 11 countries. Spraying was frequent, almost weekly for 10 to 12 months each year, in some cases over a period of 20 years. The idea was to stop transmission of the parasite for the duration of the life span of the worm in humans, considered to be more than a decade.

This ambitious programme is thought to have protected some 40 million people in West Africa from river blindness and opened up 250,000 square kilometres of land in previously infected river valleys to resettlement and cultivation. Monitoring of other insects, and fish, in the treated rivers indicated few deleterious effects, and the current view of river ecologists is that permanent damage to other creatures in these rivers is unlikely.

Global warming

The human-induced warming of the global climate has issued in a new era of society's influence on rivers. An overall increase in temperature will melt snow and ice and translate into a greater loss of moisture from soils due to higher evaporation and transpiration from plants. River flows will also be affected by changes in precipitation amounts, the intensity and duration of storms, their timing, and the type of precipitation involved. Climatologists agree that extreme weather events (examples include tropical cyclones, droughts, heat waves, and heavy rainstorms) are likely to become more frequent, more widespread, and/or more intense in many parts of the world as the 21st century progresses. All will inevitably result in changes to rivers. Less direct, but potentially no less significant, changes will also occur due to the ways in which plant communities respond to climatic warming. Societies too can be expected to increase their influence on some rivers in response to other aspects of climate change; expanding irrigation systems, for example, in regions subject to more droughts.

Detecting the impact of global warming on rivers is by no means always straightforward because of the difficulties of separating the effect of climate change from the natural variability of many fluvial characteristics and the need to take account of possible alternative causes of change, such as alterations to land use and other human activities. Nonetheless, the influence of global warming has already been identified in some recent modifications to fluvial systems. Work on a number of the world's large drainage basins has established a significant rising trend in the risk of great floods (those with a return period of 100 years) in the 20th century. Warmer air temperatures are also having a predictable effect on glaciers – melting and retreat – in many parts of the world. Glaciers are receding particularly fast in the Himalaya and parts of Tibet, generating worries about long-term water supplies for hundreds of millions of people in India, Bangladesh, Nepal, and China who rely on rivers fed by glacial meltwater.

Ice cover has been in general decline since the mid-19th century on most rivers in North America and Eurasia as gradual warming has meant freeze-up dates have been occurring later and break-up dates arriving earlier. In the case of the lower Don River in Russia, the length of the ice season has been reduced by a whole month in about 100 years. Records for the Tornionjoki River in Finland stretch back to 1692 and show a long-term trend towards earlier break-up dates throughout the entire period. This tendency is not universal, however. Rivers in central and eastern Siberia display significant trends in the opposite direction: towards longer periods with ice cover due to earlier freeze-up dates and later break-up dates.

Northern hemisphere rivers that flow into the Arctic Ocean have been delivering more water in line with longer ice-free periods, combined with an increase in precipitation. More fresh water in the Arctic could slow down or shut off the so-called 'thermohaline circulation', an oceanic current conveyor belt which transports large amounts of warm water to the North Atlantic region. This circulation is driven by differences in the density of sea water, controlled by temperature and salinity, so more fresh water could counteract the flow. The thermohaline circulation helps to regulate the climate of northern Europe, maintaining temperatures that are higher than would be otherwise expected given the latitude.

Conversely, a number of other rivers have seen declines in the amount of water they carry each year since the mid-20th century. Several of the major rivers with dwindling flows serve large populations, sparking further concerns about future water supplies. These rivers include the Yellow River in northern China, the Ganges in India, the Niger in West Africa, and the Colorado in North America.

Drought is thought to be the greatest agent of change associated with global warming in the Amazon Basin. Many computer-based models of future climate in the region indicate a reduction of dry-season rainfall, the effects of which will be exacerbated by rising air temperatures. This increased probability of drought will have all sorts of knock-on effects for the forest ecosystems and the rivers running through them, including a greater likelihood of fire. The consequences for local people, wildlife, and the rivers themselves are expected to be serious.

In Europe, the discharge of the Rhine is expected to become more seasonal because of global warming. Estimates generated by computer models indicate that by 2050, the average flow in summer will decrease by up to 45% and the average winter flow will increase by up to 30%. Less water in the Rhine during the summer months is related mainly to predicted decreases in precipitation and increases in evapotranspiration. Greater flows in winter will be caused by a combination of more precipitation, less snow storage, and increased early melting. The hazards posed by winter floods on the Rhine will certainly increase in consequence. Greater seasonality in the river's flow will also have numerous repercussions for the ecology of the Rhine.

River restoration

The numerous ways in which human activities have influenced rivers, both purposefully and indirectly, are complemented in many countries by efforts to reverse some of the earlier effects of human action: so-called 'river restoration'. Attempts to improve conditions in rivers are not new in themselves, as evidenced in the clean-up of the Thames in London cited earlier in this chapter, for instance, but the widespread adoption of restoration, rehabilitation, and mitigation measures has been recognized as a distinctive phase of river management in the late 20th and early 21st centuries. Restoration projects usually involve efforts to repair damage to rivers, typically in an attempt to better meet societies' needs and expectations for natural, ecologically healthy waterways.

Returning a river to its 'natural' or 'original' condition is usually fraught with difficulty, however. Theoretically, at least, this can be based on an understanding of historical conditions along a river before human effects, or on conditions along a similar but less affected reference river. In practice, however, an appropriate reference river may not exist, or conditions in a basin (such as climate or vegetation) may have changed since the period selected for the historical baseline. Indeed, rivers change under all sorts of natural circumstances, and determining which changes are natural and which are due to human pressures is not always straightforward. Further, although it may be possible to determine which human impacts are undesirable, preventing them entirely may be more complicated.

These and other constraints mean that re-establishing conditions that might have existed prior to human settlement of the landscape is virtually impossible. It is more appropriate to restore rivers that are self-sustaining and integrated into the surrounding landscape and are, therefore, generally closer to a more natural state. Hence, for example, the Plan Loire Grandeur Nature for the Loire River in France, one of the largest river restoration programmes undertaken anywhere, aims to ensure the conservation of typical Loire Valley ecosystems (including peatlands, gorges, alluvial forests, and oxbow lakes) on model sites and to maintain their ecological functions. Part and parcel of this effort is the re-establishment of iconic river species such as the beaver and salmon.

Even when the objectives of river restoration programmes are clear, in most cases they will still have to be balanced against other demands put on rivers. Some of these demands may be conflicting. For example, some conservationists argue that river regulation and environmental conservation are intrinsically incompatible since regulation modifies the natural environment in which original wildlife communities became established. Indeed, in certain cases, the ecological requirements of organisms are destroyed or modified beyond the limits of adaptations and the organisms are unable to survive. River management is no different from any other natural environmental management issue in that it involves compromises, and in a world where the growth of populations and economies appears to be inexorable, not to mention the all-embracing effects of human-induced climate change, these compromises are likely to become more and more delicate.

Epilogue

Virtually every reader of this book will have some sort of relationship with a river, or perhaps more than one. It may involve living on a floodplain or benefiting directly from a river's flow, maybe as an angler or via a system of plumbing. The number of ways in which rivers impinge on human society is great, and there are few places on Earth where rivers do not exert an influence, be it direct or indirect, current or historical.

The aim of this book has been to celebrate rivers in all their diversity. Bountiful yet capricious, rivers represent different things to different people, sometimes contradictory, at others complementary. They form vital components to innumerable ecosystems, and nourish both town and country. That nourishment has been spiritual as much as literal. Rivers are worshipped and revered, respected and feared. From raging torrents to babbling brooks, their waters have fuelled the thoughts of artists, scientists, philosophers, and generals. In a very real sense, much of human history has taken place on the banks of rivers.

The ancient Greek philosopher Heraclitus of Ephesus asserted that 'you cannot step twice into the same river'. All rivers are inherently dynamic. A meandering channel can abruptly become braided, or a trickle burst out of its banks to inundate a plain. So too the life they sustain, from mountain peaks to muddy deltas, on timescales ranging from the nymphal life of a mayfly to the extinction of the Yangtze river dolphin. Humankind's use and abuse of rivers has been equally diverse and vibrant, ranging from development of the earliest river boats to the choking of waterways with industrial effluent.

River channels occupy just a tiny fraction of the land surface, but their influence is out of all proportion to this immediate footprint. No matter how you may perceive rivers, all must acknowledge the wide and eclectic menu of river-based themes. Together, they reflect both the natural and social history of our planet.

Further reading

P. Ackroyd, *Thames: Sacred River* (London: Chatto & Windus, 2007).

K. J. Avery and F. Kelly, *Hudson River School Visions: The Landscapes of Sanford R. Gifford* (New York: Metropolitan Museum of Art Publications, 2003).

B. K. Belton, *Orinoco Flow: Culture, Narrative, and the Political Economy of Information* (Lanham: Scarecrow Press, 2003).

A. C. Benke and C. E. Cushing (eds.), *Rivers of North America* (Amsterdam: Academic Press, 2005).

T. M. Berra, *Freshwater Fish Distribution* (Chicago: University of Chicago Press, 2001).

I. C. Campbell (ed.), *The Mekong: Biophysical Environment of an International River Basin* (Amsterdam: Elsevier Press, 2010).

J. Cao, *China Along the Yellow River: Reflections on Rural Society* (Abingdon: Routledge Curzon, 2005).

M. Cioc, *The Rhine: An Eco-Biography, 1815–2000* (Seattle: University of Washington Press, 2002).

F. S. Colwell, *Rivermen: A Romantic Iconography of the River and the Source* (Montreal: McGill-Queen's University Press, 1989).

N. Compton, *The Battle for the Buffalo River: A Twentieth-Century Conservation Crisis in the Ozarks* (Fayetteville: University of Arkansas Press, 1992).

J. Conrad, *Heart of Darkness* (London: Penguin Classics, 1973).

S. Darby and D. Sear, *River Restoration: Managing the Uncertainty in Restoring Physical Habitat* (Chichester: Wiley, 2008).

L. de Waal, P. M. Wade, and A. Large, *Rehabilitation of Rivers: Principles and Implementation* (Chichester: Wiley, 1998).

D. Dudgeon, *Tropical Stream Ecology* (Amsterdam: Academic Press, 2008).

M. D. Evenden, *Fish Versus Power: An Environmental History of the Fraser River* (New York: Cambridge University Press, 2004).

A. Feldhaus, *Water and Womanhood: Religious Meanings of Rivers in Maharashtra* (New York: Oxford University Press, 1995).

P. Fradkin, *A River No More: The Colorado River and the West*, 2nd edn. (Berkeley: University of California Press, 1996).

P. S. Giller and B. Malmqvist, *The Biology of Streams and Rivers* (Oxford: Oxford University Press, 1998).

A. L. Godinho, B. Kynard, and H. P. Godinho, *Life in a Brazilian Floodplain River: Migration, Spawning, and Management of São Francisco River Fishes* (Saarbrücken: LAP Lambert Academic Publishing, 2010).

W. Grady (ed.), *Dark Waters Dancing to a Breeze: A Literary Companion to Rivers and Lakes* (Vancouver: Greystone Books, 2007).

S. de Gramont, *The Strong Brown God: The Story of the Niger River* (Boston: Houghton Mifflin, 1975).

A. Gupta (ed.), *Large Rivers: Geomorphology and Management* (Chichester: Wiley, 2008).

J. Harding, P. Mosley, C. Pearson, and B. Sorrell, *Freshwaters of New Zealand* (Wellington: New Zealand Hydrological Society/New Zealand Limnological Society, 2004).

S. M. Haslam, *The Riverscape and the River* (Cambridge: Cambridge University Press, 2008).

J. Hemming, *Tree of Rivers: The Story of the Amazon* (London: Thames & Hudson, 2008).

J. F. Hornig (ed.), *Social and Environmental Impacts of the James Bay Hydroelectric Project* (Montreal: McGill-Queen's University Press, 1999).

P. J. Jones, *Reading Rivers in Roman Literature and Culture* (Lanham, MD: Lexington Books, 2005).

R. Kingsford (ed.), *Ecology of Desert Rivers* (Cambridge: Cambridge University Press, 2006).

L. B. Leopold, *Water, Rivers and Creeks* (Sausalito, CA: University Science Books, 1997).

M. C. Lucas and E. Baras, *Migration of Freshwater Fishes* (Oxford: Blackwell Science, 2001).

C. Mauch and T. Zeller (eds.), *Rivers in History: Perspectives on Waterways in Europe and North America* (Pittsburgh: University of Pittsburgh Press, 2008).

A. Meadows and P. S. Meadows (eds.), *The Indus River: Biodiversity, Resources, Humankind* (Karachi: Oxford University Press, 1999).

M. Meybeck, G. de Marsilly, and E. Fustec (eds.), *La Seine en son Bassin: Fonctionnement écologique d'un système fluvial anthropisé* (Paris: Elsevier, 1998).

S. Mithen and E. Black, *Water, Life and Civilisation: Climate, Environment and Society in the Jordan Valley* (Cambridge: Cambridge University Press, 2011).

C. Morris, *The Big Muddy: An Environmental History of the Mississippi and Its Peoples, from Hernando de Soto to Hurricane Katrina* (New York: Oxford University Press, 2010).

P. K. Parua, *The Ganga: Water Use in the Indian Subcontinent* (Dordrecht: Springer, 2010).

A. Poiani (ed.), *Floods in an Arid Continent, Advances in Ecological Research* 39 (San Diego: Academic Press, 2006).

J. D. Priscoli and A.T. Wolf, *Managing and Transforming Water Conflicts* (Cambridge: Cambridge University Press, 2009).

R. Randolph Ashton, *A Celebration of Salmon Rivers* (Mechanicsburg: Stackpole Books, 2007).

C. W. Sadoff, D. Whittington, and D. Grey, *Africa's International Rivers: An Economic Perspective* (Washington, DC: World Bank, 2002).

R. Said, *The River Nile: Geology, Hydrology and Utilization* (Oxford: Elsevier Science, 1993).

S. M. A. Salman and K. Uprety, *Conflict and Cooperation on South Asia's International Rivers: A Legal Perspective* (Washington, DC: World Bank, 2002).

S. A. Schumm, *River Variability and Complexity* (Cambridge: Cambridge University Press, 2005).

T. Scudder, *The Future of Large Dams* (London: Earthscan, 2006).

P. Sinclair, *The Murray: A River and its People* (Carlton South: Melbourne University Press, 2001).

D. E. Spritzer, *Waters of Wealth: The Story of the Kootenai River and Libby Dam* (Boulder: Pruett, 1979).

K. Tockner, U. Uehlinger, and C. T. Robinson (eds.), *Rivers of Europe* (Amsterdam: Academic Press, 2009).

S. Turvey, *Witness to Extinction: How We Failed to Save the Yangtze River Dolphin* (Oxford: Oxford University Press, 2008).

E. E. Wohl, *A World of Rivers: Environmental Change on Ten of the World's Great Rivers* (Chicago: University of Chicago Press, 2010).

Further reading

Index

Expand your collection of
VERY SHORT INTRODUCTIONS

1. Classics
2. Music
3. Buddhism
4. Literary Theory
5. Hinduism
6. Psychology
7. Islam
8. Politics
9. Theology
10. Archaeology
11. Judaism
12. Sociology
13. The Koran
14. The Bible
15. Social and Cultural Anthropology
16. History
17. Roman Britain
18. The Anglo-Saxon Age
19. Medieval Britain
20. The Tudors
21. Stuart Britain
22. Eighteenth-Century Britain
23. Nineteenth-Century Britain
24. Twentieth-Century Britain
25. Heidegger
26. Ancient Philosophy
27. Socrates
28. Marx
29. Logic
30. Descartes
31. Machiavelli
32. Aristotle
33. Hume
34. Nietzsche
35. Darwin
36. The European Union
37. Gandhi
38. Augustine
39. Intelligence
40. Jung
41. Buddha
42. Paul
43. Continental Philosophy
44. Galileo
45. Freud
46. Wittgenstein
47. Indian Philosophy
48. Rousseau
49. Hegel
50. Kant
51. Cosmology
52. Drugs
53. Russian Literature
54. The French Revolution
55. Philosophy
56. Barthes
57. Animal Rights
58. Kierkegaard
59. Russell
60. Shakespeare
61. Clausewitz
62. Schopenhauer
63. The Russian Revolution

GEOGRAPHY
A Very Short Introduction
John A. Matthews & David T. Herbert

Modern Geography has come a long way from its historical roots in exploring foreign lands, and simply mapping and naming the regions of the world. Spanning both physical and human Geography, the discipline today is unique as a subject which can bridge the divide between the sciences and the humanities, and between the environment and our society. Using wide-ranging examples from global warming and oil, to urbanization and ethnicity, this *Very Short Introduction* paints a broad picture of the current state of Geography, its subject matter, concepts and methods, and its strengths and controversies. The book's conclusion is no less than a manifesto for Geography's future.

'Matthews and Herbert's book is written—as befits the VSI series—in an accessible prose style and is peppered with attractive and understandable images, graphs and tables.'

Geographical.

LANDSCAPES AND GEOMORPHOLOGY
A Very Short Introduction
Andrew Goudie & Heather Viles

Landscapes are all around us, but most of us know very little about how they have developed, what goes on in them, and how they react to changing climates, tectonics and human activities. Examining what landscape is, and how we use a range of ideas and techniques to study it, Andrew Goudie and Heather Viles demonstrate how geomorphologists have built on classic methods pioneered by some great 19th century scientists to examine our Earth. Using examples from around the world, including New Zealand, the Tibetan Plateau, and the deserts of the Middle East, they examine some of the key controls on landscape today such as tectonics and climate, as well as humans and the living world.

www.oup.com/vsi